5 Ingredient Favourites

Grace Mortimer

5 Ingredient Favourites

Delicious easy meals to feed the whole family

HQ

Contents

Introduction

I love cooking! I know not everyone does, but I do. I love the day just before a food shop when my fridge is all but empty and my cupboards are looking a little sparse. Why? When I realise I've only got a few simple ingredients to work with, I actually relish the challenge of coming up with a delicious meal, making it up as I go along.

I'm a busy mum who is often clattering around in the kitchen to the sound of, '*Can I have something to eat, Mummy? I'm hungry!*' Speed is often a factor. But amidst the chaos of life, what greater reward is there than throwing something together that turns out to be an absolutely cracking meal, enjoyed by all and seemingly produced from nothing! From my bonkers kitchen to yours, this is a collection of those recipes. And I set myself three criteria:

1. **Using no more than five ingredients**

2. **Naturally nutritious**

3. **Budget-friendly**

They don't require special gadgets and can mostly be cooked in batches, so there's little or no waste. I hate throwing food away; it feels like chucking money in the bin. Whether you are on a tight budget or have simply become bored with eating the same things, I hope this serves as the least intimidating cookbook you own! Each meal consists of basic staples that you probably either have already, or won't cost much to buy.

Included are tips and tricks to make the most from basic but delicious ingredients, to use leftovers and reduce food waste, and – most importantly – eat homemade, balanced meals that are full of flavour.

Shopping List

My main advice when shopping for the basics is to steer clear of the branded stuff! Chopped tomatoes are chopped tomatoes are chopped tomatoes. You don't need to buy the posh ones in black tins with fancy writing! Often, supermarkets run offers on branded items, such as 'buy 4 for the price of 3' or similar, but if you do the maths, four tins of the unbranded alternative still work out cheaper – and that's if you actually need four tins of the same thing! Those special offer labels are very inviting for a reason, but the best way to reduce overall spending on your weekly food shop is to plan what you're going to cook and start with the supermarket's own basics range. These are often on the bottom or top shelf (i.e., not at direct eyeline height). That's not to say you should never buy branded items – I think we all have our favourite brand of coffee or chocolate (I do, at least!) – but for the staples, this is a great way to reduce spending and eat just as well.

Cupboard essentials

- Self-raising flour
- Basmati rice
- Curry powder
- Coconut milk
- Tinned chickpeas
- Tinned chopped tomatoes
- Paprika
- Ground cinnamon
- Porridge oats
- Pasta
- Lentils
- Tinned tuna
- Potatoes
- Eggs
- Tinned butter beans
- Bread
- Pesto

Fridge

- Cheese
- Milk
- Beef mince
- Plain yoghurt
- Bacon
- Chicken
- Cream cheese
- Chorizo
- Cauliflower
- Peppers
- Double cream
- Courgettes

Freezer

- Peas
- Mixed veg
- Spinach
- Sweetcorn

Useful equipment

- Slow cooker
- Stick blender/food processor
- Muffin tin
- Large ovenproof dish
- Loaf tin
- Loose-bottomed cake tin

Key to symbols

V Vegetarian

F Suitable for freezing

Breakfast

V F

blueberry & vanilla pancakes

Makes
8

What's not to love? These are very versatile. For those who don't eat eggs, the egg can swapped for chia egg (see Tip), and the blueberries can be swapped for raspberries or strawberries, but there's something about the colour of blueberry pancakes that makes them so beautiful, especially when they are drizzled with some glistening syrup – yum!

130g (1 cup/4½oz) self-raising flour

250ml (1 cup) milk

(any type)

1 egg

1 handful of blueberries, plus extra (optional) to serve

1 tsp vanilla extract

For cooking

drizzle of sunflower oil

1. Combine all the ingredients, except the oil, in a bowl and beat thoroughly until well combined.
2. Heat a drizzle of oil in a frying pan over a medium heat. Add ladle-sized amounts of the mixture to the frying pan and fry on each side for a couple of minutes until golden.
3. Serve immediately, with more blueberries and a drizzle of syrup if you wish.
4. Fine to freeze. To cook from frozen, allow the pancakes to defrost naturally, then reheat in the microwave or in a dry frying pan.

Tip

To make a chia egg, simply mix 1 level tablespoon of chia seeds with 2 tablespoons of water and set aside for 10 minutes to allow the chia seeds to swell and become jelly-like in consistency. Add it to the pancake mixture, as you would an egg.

V F

melt-in-the-middle muffins

Makes
6

These muffins have melted cheese in the middle. Need I say more?!

3 handfuls of spinach

130g (1 cup/4½oz) self-raising flour

4 tbsp milk (any type)

3 eggs

6 small cubes of Cheddar cheese

For greasing

butter or sunflower oil

1. Preheat the oven to 200°C (180°C fan). Grease a 6-hole muffin tin with a little butter or oil.
2. Finely chop the spinach and place it in a bowl along with the flour, milk and eggs. Beat thoroughly to break up any lumps.
3. Pour the mixture into the holes of the muffin tin and push one cube of cheese into the middle of each muffin.
4. Bake for 30 minutes.
5. Remove from the oven and leave to cool slightly before popping them out to enjoy.
6. Fine to freeze. Defrost naturally and reheat in the microwave or pop them in a 200°C (180°C fan) oven for 10 minutes.

V F

black forest gateau pancakes

Makes
16–18

Cherries and melted chocolate, it doesn't get much more indulgent than that for breakfast. These could just as easily be served as a dessert.

½ x 400g (14oz) tin of cherry pie filling, plus extra (optional) to serve

1 egg

200g (1½ cups/7oz) self-raising flour

250ml (1 cup) milk

1 handful of chocolate chips, plus extra (optional) to serve

For cooking

drizzle of sunflower oil

1. Combine all the ingredients in a bowl and mix thoroughly.
2. Heat a drizzle of oil in a frying pan over a medium heat, then add the mixture in ladle-sized amounts, spaced apart. Cook the pancakes for a couple of minutes on each side or until golden.
3. Serve topped with the remaining cherry pie filling, and extra chocolate chips, if you wish.

V F

baked bean waffles

Serves
2

Yes, you read that right! And, yes, they are this bright! The first time I made these and shared the recipe online, the feedback was unbelievable. Baked beans are marvellous but they can be a little messy just served on their own. When cooked like this, however, they break down and become almost creamy. You just have to try it for yourself.

about 4 tbsp tinned baked beans

1 tbsp plain yoghurt

3 tbsp self-raising flour

1 handful of grated cheese (any type)

1 tbsp tomato purée

For greasing

butter or sunflower oil

1. Preheat the oven to 200°C (180°C fan). Prepare a silicone waffle mould, about 18.5 x 18.5 x 1.5cm (7 x 7 x ¾in) or grease a 6-hole muffin tin with a little butter or oil.
2. Mix all the ingredients together in a bowl until well combined. Spoon the mixture into the waffle mould or muffin tin.
3. Bake for 30 minutes.
4. Remove from the oven and leave until nearly cool before popping them out to serve.
5. Fine to freeze. To cook from frozen, defrost naturally, then reheat in the microwave for 30 seconds.

Tip *You can, of course, use a waffle iron to cook these. Grease it beforehand and follow the manufacturer's instructions. You will find that they cook much more quickly, and you may need to loosen the mixture with a little extra milk.*

V F

cheesy cereal muffins

Makes
6

Cheese and cereal ... What?! Please don't be put off by what sounds like a truly bizarre combination, because you'll be missing out on these lovely muffins. Think of the wheat bicuits as being like breadcrumbs with less salt and more fibre. Now, perhaps, this recipe doesn't seem as strange to you as it once did. These are so moist and delicious, you'll just have to trust me on this and give them a go for yourself!

1 courgette

1 wheat biscuit (such as Weetabix)

2 handfuls of grated cheese (any type), plus 6 extra cubes of cheese for topping (optional)

2 eggs

For greasing

butter or sunflower oil

1. Preheat the oven to 200°C (180°C fan). Grease a 6-hole muffin tin with a little butter or oil, or fill the holes with paper muffin cases.
2. Grate the courgette into a bowl and crumble in the wheat biscuit. Add the grated cheese and eggs and mix thoroughly.
3. Spoon the mixture into the muffin tin holes or cases and squash it down with the back of a spoon. If you like, you can also add an extra cube of cheese to the top of each muffin.
4. Bake for 35 minutes.
5. Remove from the oven and leave to cool, then serve.
6. Fine to freeze. To cook from frozen, defrost naturally, then reheat in the microwave for 20–30 seconds.

V F

apple pie porridge

Serves
2–3

Dark winter mornings call for hot, sweet, spiced porridge, in my opinion, and this is just that.

100g (1 cup/3½oz) porridge oats

3 tbsp apple sauce from a jar, plus extra (optional) to serve

1 tbsp brown sugar

1 tsp ground cinnamon

250ml (1 cup) milk

1. Add everything to a saucepan over a low heat and simmer for 10 minutes, stirring occasionally to prevent it from sticking. That's it!

Tip *I like to serve this with an extra dollop of apple sauce on top.*

V F

blueberry porridge pies

Makes **6**

These are soft and squidgy, with a burst of fruit inside. They make a comforting start to the day and are a considerably less messy way to serve porridge (which, as we all know, turns to concrete if left to go cold!). If you're in a rush, these are great for breakfast on-the-go or alternatively are very nice dipped in thick, full-fat yoghurt mixed with a few extra blueberries for good measure.

100g (1 cup/3½oz) porridge oats

250ml (1 cup) milk (any type)

1 egg

1 handful of blueberries

3 tbsp apple sauce

For greasing

butter or sunflower oil

1. Preheat the oven to 200°C (180°C fan). Grease a 6-hole muffin tin with a little butter or oil or fill the holes with paper muffin cases.
2. Combine the oats, milk and egg in a bowl and mix thoroughly. Pour the mixture into the prepared muffin tin holes or cases.
3. Mash the blueberries and divide them equally among each muffin, then add an equal-sized dollop of apple sauce on top.
4. Bake for 30 minutes.
5. Remove from the oven and leave them to nearly cool before popping them out.
6. Fine to freeze. Simply defrost to eat.

V

cheesy tomato eggs in a hole

Makes
1

If you've got some slightly stale slices of bread (or perhaps the end slices that no one really opts for), this is a great way to bring them back to life and ensure they get eaten! Best served with ketchup, in my opinion. Yum!

1 slice of bread

1 tbsp tomato purée

1 egg

1 small handful of grated cheese (any type)

1. Preheat the oven to 200°C (180°C fan).
2. Take the bread and place it on a baking tray lined with baking parchment, then use the bottom of a glass to squash down a circular imprint into the middle of the bread.
3. Spread the tomato purée over the whole slice. Crack the egg into the circular well you've made in the bread, then cover the whole slice with the cheese.
4. Bake for 15 minutes (or alternatively pop it in the air fryer at 200°C for 10 minutes). You'll know when the egg is cooked through because it puffs up out of the well.

V F

blueberry & lemon baked oats

Serves
4

A classic flavour combination for a reason, and delicious served with a generous helping of thick Greek yoghurt.

100g (1 cup/3½oz) blueberries

160g (½ cup/5½oz) lemon curd

200g (2 cups/7oz) porridge oats

2 eggs

250ml (1 cup) milk

For greasing

butter or sunflower oil

1. Preheat the oven to 200°C (180°C fan). Grease an ovenproof dish.
2. Add all the ingredients to the ovenproof dish, mix thoroughly, then bake in the oven for 30 minutes.
3. Once cooked, remove from the oven and leave to cool for 15–20 minutes before spooning into portions.

V F

chocolate button-stuffed pancakes

Makes
8–10

Stuffed pancakes sound like there might be some elaborate process that involves piping equipment and many, many bowls, but this recipe is anything but complicated.

180g (1⅓ cups/6oz) self-raising flour

200ml (¾ cup) milk

1 egg

giant chocolate buttons

For cooking

drizzle of sunflower oil or knob of butter

1. Combine the flour, milk and egg in a bowl and use a whisk to mix together well, ensuring there are no lumps. The batter should be quite thick.

2. Heat a drizzle of oil or butter in a frying pan over a medium heat, then add tablespoon-sized amounts of the batter to the pan, spaced apart. You want a thick dollop that spreads rather than runs.

3. Immediately place a chocolate button in the middle of each pancake, then spoon over another tablespoon of pancake batter to cover and cook for a minute or two. Once bubbles start to appear on the top of the pancakes, they are ready to flip. Turn over and fry on the other side for a couple of minutes or until golden.

4. Serve!

Soups & Salads

V

avocado & apricot salad with raspberry dressing

Serves
3

Children and salad. Not a likely duo, but don't dismiss the possibility just yet. Whether it's barbecue weather or not, this brightly coloured bowl of goodness is absolutely delicious and goes well with the finest burnt sausage or skewer around.

1 avocado, peeled and de-stoned
4 fresh ripe apricots
2 handfuls of raspberries
1 ball of mozzarella
glug of olive oil

1. Slice the avocado and apricots into wedges and place them in a serving bowl, with half the raspberries.
2. Tear up chunks of the mozzarella and pop them on top of the avocado, apricots and raspberries.
3. Mash the remaining raspberries in a separate bowl with a fork. Add a glug of olive oil to the raspberries and whisk in with the fork.
4. Pour the raspberry dressing over the salad and it's ready to serve.

V

pear & parsnip soup

Serves **2**

It shouldn't work, but it does! Beige, sweet, creamy and comforting – this is one you'll just have to trust me and try.

- 1 parsnip
- knob of butter
- 1 low-salt vegetable or chicken stock cube
- 1 pear
- 2 tbsp double cream

1. Peel and chop the parsnip into small chunks. Add it to a saucepan with the knob of butter, and cook over a medium heat, allowing it to sweat down for 10 minutes.
2. Meanwhile, boil the kettle.
3. Measure out 500ml (2 cups) of boiling water, add the stock cube and mix, then pour it into the saucepan. Simmer until the parsnip is soft.
4. Using a stick blender, blitz the parsnip and stock until smooth.
5. Peel and chop the pear and add it to the saucepan. Simmer until the pear turns soft.
6. Once again, blitz until smooth.
7. Stir in the double cream and that's it. It's ready to serve.

Tip *Swirl in some olive oil or extra cream and sprinkle with black pepper to make a little more indulgent.*

'forget the lettuce' salad

Serves
4

When you think of salad, it can conjure up images of wilting lettuce leaves and you probably assume it's an accompaniment to something much tastier and more filling. Well, this is the main event and no one is going to be hungry after a bowl of it! Packed with protein and pretty as a picture, even your kids might eat it. Although don't tell them it's a salad, would be my advice.

1 x 750g (1lb 10½oz) bag of miniature potatoes

1 handful of trimmed green beans

2 eggs

2 handfuls of cherry tomatoes, halved

1 x 145g (5oz) tin of tuna, drained

To finish

drizzle of olive oil

1. Add the potatoes to a large pan of boiling water and cook for 15 minutes. Halfway through cooking, add the green beans and drop the eggs in by gently lowering them into the water using a tablespoon to prevent them from cracking.

2. After 15 minutes, drain everything, running the eggs under cold water to cool and stop cooking. Once cool, peel the eggs.

3. Arrange the potatoes and green beans in a large salad dish along with the tomatoes and flaked tuna. Slice or quarter the boiled eggs and add them on top. Drizzle over a little olive oil and season if you wish.

V F

starts with a tin – minestrone

Serves **4**

This is a great option to have in your arsenal for when you've got literally nothing in the fridge to eat! Made from entirely tinned and cupboard ingredients, the likes of which you've probably got hanging around anyway, my advice would be this: remember you glanced across this recipe when you first opened the book, and make a mental note of it for that day before you're due a food shop and you've somehow got to produce a meal out of thin air. You can thank me later.

1 x 400g (14oz) tin of vegetable soup

1 x 400g (14oz) tin of chopped tomatoes

80g (3oz) pasta shapes

1 low-salt vegetable stock cube, crumbled

150g (1 cup/5oz) frozen mixed veg

1. Add everything to a large saucepan along with 500ml (2 cups) of boiling water and simmer for 15 minutes (or until the pasta is cooked).

2. And that's it. Go ahead and serve!

MICROWAVE
Do not reheat.
INGREDIENTS Water

V

german potato salad

Serves
4

Tom, my partner, is German, and when we first got together I made a potato salad to accompany a barbecue we were hosting for family. He took one look at it and asked me quite innocently, 'Where are the gherkins?' I was puzzled by this. It turns out it wasn't a German potato salad if it didn't have gherkins in it! In due course he made potato salad the way he felt it should be made and, honestly, it's a revelation!

250g (9oz) potatoes, chopped into bite-sized chunks

3 eggs

3 gherkins (plus 3 tbsp pickling juice), finely sliced

2 spring onions, finely sliced

110g (½ cup/4oz) mayonnaise

1. Add the potatoes to a large saucepan of boiling water along with the eggs, then add a good pinch of salt. Boil for approximately 12 minutes (or until the potatoes are soft but still holding their shape). Drain and set aside to cool.
2. To assemble the sauce, add the sliced gherkins and spring onions to a bowl. Spoon in the mayonnaise and add 3 good tablespoons of the pickling juice from the gherkins, then beat the sauce together with a fork until it is a pourable consistency (add more gherkin juice if necessary). Season with salt and pepper if you wish.
3. Once the potatoes are warm, tip them into a bowl. Peel and roughly chop or quarter the eggs and sprinkle them over the potatoes. Pour over the sauce and tumble the salad together to evenly combine. That's it!

V F

roasted tomato & garlic soup with croutons

Serves
4

Soup always sounds like a faff to my mind, but this is basically a roast that you blitz up at the end – and it's delicious. You can reduce the amount of garlic if you plan on being in close proximity to any other human beings in the following days, but I would probably offer them a bowl of it and deal with the problem that way. It's up to you.

1 bulb of garlic, cloves peeled

500g (1lb 2oz) tomatoes, halved

2 red onions, cut into quarters

1 low-salt vegetable stock cube

2 slices of bread, torn into pieces

For cooking

olive oil

1. Preheat the oven to 200°C (180°C fan).
2. Add the garlic cloves to a large baking tray lined with baking parchment, along with the tomatoes, onions and a drizzle of oil. Bake for 30 minutes.
3. Remove the tray from the oven, but leave the oven on, and add the veg to a food processor along with the crumbled stock cube and 500ml (2 cups) of boiling water. Blitz until smooth. Season if you wish.
4. Transfer the soup to a saucepan and gently bring to a simmer.
5. Meanwhile, in the same tray as the vegetables were roasted in, remove the baking parchment, wipe with kitchen towel to remove any excess moisture and add the bread along with a good drizzle of oil. Bake for 10 minutes, then remove and sprinkle over the soup. Top it off with black pepper and serve.

V

tuscan bread salad

Serves
4

It was my partner Tom who first introduced me to this. He asked me if I'd ever tried 'bread salad', to which I laughed and assumed he was pulling my leg. Then he produced it to serve alongside some fish and I couldn't believe I'd never heard of it before. Completely delicious, very moreish and full of different textures and complementary flavours.

2 stale ciabatta rolls, cut into chunks

1 handful of cherry tomatoes, halved

1 red onion, sliced

1 handful of pitted black olives

1 bunch of basil leaves

To finish

drizzle of olive oil

1. Add the bread chunks to a large salad dish.

2. Sprinkle the tomatoes and red onion with a little salt, then leave them to partially pickle for 10 minutes before adding them to the bread chunks. Add the olives and basil leaves, toss together and drizzle over a little olive oil. You're finished!

Tip *If you don't have stale bread, just slice the bread, pop it on a tray and bake for 10 minutes at 180°C (160°C fan).*

Easy Wins

chicken & spinach alfredo

Serves
4

Melted Parmesan in cream with pasta – how could you say no?!

2 skinless and boneless chicken breasts, diced

300ml (1¼ cups) double cream

2 handfuls of grated Parmesan

250g (9oz) pasta shapes

100g (3½oz) spinach leaves

For cooking

drizzle of sunflower oil

1. Heat a drizzle of oil in a frying pan over a medium heat, and fry the chicken breasts until golden. Then add the double cream and half the Parmesan and turn the heat down to low.

2. Meanwhile, cook the pasta in a pan of boiling water according to the packet instructions, then drain.

3. Once the pasta is cooked, add it to the chicken along with the spinach and remaining Parmesan and mix. Turn off the heat and leave for a couple of minutes to allow the Parmesan to melt and the spinach to soften slightly. Season if you wish.

V

caprese tart

Serves
4

Caprese is a combination of tomatoes, mozzarella and basil and it's a classic for a reason! This is basically just turning a caprese salad into a 'pizza' (to children's ears) or a 'tart' (to any adults wondering how you made it and whether they could have the recipe) but with the addition of delicious pesto because, why not?

1 sheet of ready-made puff pastry
3 tbsp pesto
3–4 tomatoes, sliced
1 ball of mozzarella
a few basil leaves

For brushing

1 beaten egg or a little milk

1. Preheat the oven to 200°C (180°C fan).
2. On a baking tray lined with baking parchment, roll out the puff pastry and score a line all the way around about 2cm (¾in) from the outside.
3. Spoon the pesto into the middle and spread all the way around the pastry, being careful not to go over the line you've made. Arrange the tomatoes all over the pesto-covered pastry, then tear the mozzarella into chunks and place it in the gaps. Brush the exposed pastry edge with the beaten egg or milk, then bake for 25 minutes.
4. Remove from the oven, tear the basil leaves across the top of the tart, slice and serve!

Tip *This recipe is veggie if you use vegetarian pesto!*

V

sundried tomato pasta

Serves
4

If 'quick' is the priority, this is a recipe you'll need; try once and you'll never flick back to this page because you'll know it off by heart immediately, as it only needs three ingredients! It's on a regular rotation in my house and if you have any of the sauce left over, it doubles up as a delicious dip or spread in sandwiches.

250g (9oz) spaghetti

1 x 250g (9oz) jar of sundried tomatoes in oil

1 handful of grated Parmesan (or vegetarian hard cheese)

1. Cook the spaghetti in a pan of boiling water according to the packet instructions. Drain, reserving a little pasta water, and return the cooked spaghetti to the saucepan.
2. Meanwhile, in a food processor, blitz the sundried tomatoes and their oil until smooth.
3. Pour the tomato mixture over the cooked pasta, along with the Parmesan and reserved pasta water. Mix thoroughly and serve immediately!

Tip *This dish is vegetarian if you use veggie Parmesan!*

V F

courgette & feta quiche

Serves
6–8

I love quiche. It looks like something that is complicated to produce, but in actual fact it is incredibly easy to make. Plus, it's a great thing to make in advance and keep in the fridge for a few days to be eaten hot or cold if you need a quick lunch. This is a delicious combination and looks beautiful once cooked.

1 sheet of ready-made shortcrust pastry
200g (7oz) feta cheese, crumbled
1 courgette, grated
3 eggs
300ml (1¼ cups) double cream

For greasing

butter or sunflower oil

1. Preheat the oven to 200°C (180°C fan).
2. Place the pastry into a well-greased, loose-bottomed 23cm (9in) tart tin and push it gently into all the edges to ensure it fits. Trim the pastry, leaving a few centimetres hanging over the edge all the way around. Using a fork, prick the pastry base and bake the pastry case for 10 minutes.
3. Meanwhile, combine the feta, courgette, eggs and cream in a bowl and whisk together. Season if you wish.
4. After 10 minutes, remove the pastry case from the oven and pour in the filling mixture. Pop the whole thing back in the oven for 35 minutes.
5. Remove from the oven, then leave to cool in the tin for 20 minutes before popping it out of its case and slicing.

V

creamy broccoli stalk pasta

Serves
4

Don't throw away the stalk when you're trimming broccoli; it's much less bitter than its fellow dark green florets and makes a lovely, thick, creamy sauce for pasta when blitzed up together. This is also a great way to reduce food waste, up the vitamins in the overall dish and create twice as much sauce from one vegetable.

400g (14oz) pasta shapes

1 head of broccoli, chopped into florets

1 tbsp pesto

100g (3½oz) cream cheese

1 handful of grated Parmesan (or vegetarian hard cheese)

1. Cook the pasta in a pan of boiling water according to the packet instructions. Drain, reserving a little of the pasta cooking water, and set aside.

2. Meanwhile, in a separate saucepan of water, boil the broccoli chunks – the pasta and broccoli will take the same time to cook.

3. Drain the broccoli and add it to a food processor along with the pesto, cream cheese and Parmesan. Blitz until smooth.

4. Combine the pasta, reserved pasta water and sauce. Give it a good mix and serve!

Tip *This dish is vegetarian if you use veggie Parmesan and pesto!*

V F

spanakopita

Makes
6–8

I first had these in Greece many years ago and I always buy one if I see them. They are a little fiddly the first time you make them but they are so worth the effort. You can omit the nutmeg if you don't have any, but it adds a lovely warm nutty spice to the finished pastries and, apart from anything else, it makes your kitchen smell amazing when cooking!

250g (9oz) spinach leaves

100g (3½oz) feta cheese, crumbled

1 egg

pinch of grated nutmeg

6–8 sheets of ready-made filo pastry

For brushing

sunflower oil

1. Preheat the oven to 200°C (180°C fan).
2. Wilt the spinach for a couple of minutes in a lidded saucepan with 2 tablespoons of cold water. Once it has cooked down, drain and finely chop it. Add it to a large bowl and allow to cool for 10 minutes. After which, add the feta, egg and nutmeg and mix until combined.
3. Lay a pastry sheet out flat, brush the whole thing with oil, then add a handful of the mixture in a long horizontal line down one side of it. Roll the pastry into one long sausage and gently curl it into a pinwheel, starting from one end. Place the whole thing on a baking tray lined with baking parchment and brush once more with oil. Repeat this process until all the spinach mixture has been used and lay all the pinwheels on the tray (not touching). Place the tray in the oven and cook for 25 minutes.
4. Remove, slice and serve while hot!

V

lemon linguine

Serves
4

I make this with linguine because I like the alliteration, but you can of course make this with any random pasta you have lying around. It's bright, fresh and delicious and is a lovely accompaniment to barbecued or slow-cooked meat.

250g (9oz) linguine

110g (½ cup/4oz) crème fraîche

zest of 1 lemon and juice of ½

1 handful of grated Parmesan (or vegetarian hard cheese)

1 handful of chopped parsley

1. Cook the linguine in a pan of boiling water according to the packet instructions, Drain, reserving a little of the pasta cooking water, and return the pasta to the saucepan.

2. To the cooked linguine, add the crème fraîche, lemon zest and juice. Sprinkle over the Parmesan, parsley and the reserved pasta water and mix thoroughly. You're ready to serve!

Tip *This dish is vegetarian if you use veggie Parmesan!*

V F

refried bean burritos

Serves
4

When I say these are seriously filling, I really mean it! Earthy spiced beans, tangy melted cheese and crunchy, slightly caramelised veg in warm tortilla breads make for a perfect quick lunch. I find there's also something really comforting about peeling off the foil to eat them.

- 1 red onion, sliced
- 1 red pepper, sliced
- 1 x 400g (14oz) tin of refried beans
- 4 tortilla wraps
- 1 handful of grated cheese (any type)

For cooking

drizzle of sunflower oil

1. Heat a drizzle of oil in a frying pan over a medium heat. Add the onion and pepper and fry until they have a little colour on them, then add the refried beans. Turn the heat down to low and allow the mixture to come to a gentle simmer. You might need to add a little water to keep it from drying out. Season if you wish. Then turn the heat off and leave the mix to thicken slightly.

2. Spoon the mixture equally into the centre of each tortilla wrap, sprinkle the cheese over the top of each one and roll into burritos. Wrap in foil if you want to keep them warm or to make them easier for holding.

prawn & sundried tomato spaghetti

Serves
4

This might be a quick meal but it's very indulgent and utterly delicious. You're basically letting the whipped garlicky cheese do all the hard work for you flavour-wise, and I won't tell anyone if you don't!

250g (9oz) spaghetti

1 handful of raw peeled prawns

1 handful of frozen peas

1 handful of chopped sundried tomatoes

75g (3oz) garlic and herb roulé cheese

For cooking

drizzle of sunflower oil

1. Cook the spaghetti in a pan of boiling water according to the packet instructions. Drain, reserving a little of the pasta cooking water, and set aside.
2. Add the prawns to a frying pan with a little oil and cook until pink and a little crispy in places. Then add the peas, sundried tomatoes and cheese along with the reserved pasta water and, using a spatula or wooden spoon, mix together until the cheese has melted to form a thick sauce.
3. Tip in the cooked spaghetti, mix thoroughly and you're ready to serve!

F

my first curry

Serves
1

When you think of curry, you probably imagine you've got to whizz to the supermarket to buy seventeen different spices you'll never use again and that's if you actually find the ones you went for in the first place. Well, this recipe calls for just one and it's probably the one you've already got! It's great to expose little ones to spices from an early age because spice doesn't necessarily mean 'spicy' and if you're hoping to raise an adventurous little foodie, this is a good place to start. Exposure is key. This recipe is great for smuggling in a few extra veggies you have lying around and takes about 15 minutes from start to finish.

1 handful of chopped skinless and boneless chicken breast (or Quorn, tofu or prawns)

1 tsp mild curry powder

1 tbsp tomato purée

½ x 400g (14oz) tin of full-fat coconut milk

cooked rice, to serve (optional)

For cooking

drizzle of sunflower oil

1. Place the chicken (or other main ingredient) in a saucepan along with the curry powder and oil and stir over a medium heat. When the chicken (or other main ingredient) is thoroughly coated in the curry powder and starting to catch at the bottom of the pan, add the tomato purée and cook for 1 minute.

2. Add the coconut milk and simmer for about 10 minutes, stirring occasionally.

3. That's it! Serve, ideally spooned over hot rice.

kedgeree

Serves
4

Kedgeree is a dish that's usually associated with breakfast, but it makes a quick and wholesome dinner, too, packed with protein and vitamins from the fish, eggs and peas. It's also really nice with a dollop of mango chutney and some warm naan breads. Mango chutney with fish, I hear you ask? Yes, mango chutney with fish.

3 eggs
1 handful of frozen peas
2 tbsp curry powder
500g (1lb 2oz) cooked rice (250g/9oz uncooked rice)
2 smoked mackerel fillets

For cooking

drizzle of sunflower oil

1. Place the eggs in a saucepan of boiling water and boil for 6 minutes (or longer, depending on how hard-boiled/runny you want the yolks). Remove and run the eggs under cold water until cool enough to peel.

2. Add the peas to a frying pan along with the curry powder and a good drizzle of oil. Tip in the cooked rice and give it a good mix. Finally, tear the mackerel into chunks and add it to the pan. Give it one final mix (not too aggressively or the mackerel will break up completely), then quarter the boiled eggs and pop them on top. Season if you wish before serving.

Tip *The rice can be precooked from a packet if you like!*

lemony bacon & broad bean pasta

Serves
4

This is instantly gratifying comfort food, in my opinion. It's delicious hot and cold and could easily be made in advance.

250g (9oz) tagliatelle or linguine

4 rashers of bacon, finely diced

170g (1 cup/6oz) broad beans

100g (3½oz) cream cheese

juice of ½ lemon

For cooking

drizzle of sunflower oil

1. Cook the pasta in a pan of boiling water according to the packet instructions. Drain, reserving a little of the pasta cooking water, and set aside.
2. While the pasta is cooking, add the bacon to a frying pan with a little oil over a medium heat. Fry until crispy then add the broad beans, cream cheese, reserved pasta water and lemon juice and mix until it forms a creamy sauce.
3. Tip the pasta into the pan and mix thoroughly until combined. You're ready to serve!

F

bologneese pinwheels

Serves
4

Spag Bol is an absolute staple in our house. When all else failed, I could guarantee that my son, Harry, would eat it. However, it usually involved an industrial clean up afterwards: stain-remover, a mop, maybe having to repaint the walls, and that's not including the orange child needing a bath! This method of delivery is considerably less messy and easier for small hands that may or may not have got the hang of cutlery yet.

500g (1lb 2oz) beef mince

3 carrots, grated

2 handfuls of chopped cherry tomatoes

1 sheet of ready-made puff pastry

2 handfuls of grated cheese (any type)

For cooking

butter or sunflower oil

For brushing

1 beaten egg or a little milk

1. Heat a little butter or oil in a pan over a medium heat, add the mince and cook until browned. Add the carrots, tomatoes and 250ml (1 cup) of boiling water and simmer for 20 minutes, or until all the water has evaporated, stirring occasionally. Season to taste if you wish, then leave to cool.
2. Preheat the oven to 200°C (180°C fan). Line a baking tray with baking parchment.
3. Unroll the pastry and spoon the cooled sauce over the whole sheet. Sprinkle over the cheese (or see Tip below). Roll up the pastry to form a sausage (not too tightly). Chop the sausage into discs, each about 2.5cm (1in) thick, and lay them flat on the prepared baking tray.
4. Brush with either milk or beaten egg. Bake for 25 minutes.
5. Remove from the oven and they're ready to serve.
6. Fine to freeze. Defrost naturally and then pop them in a 200°C (180°C fan) oven on a lined baking tray to reheat.

Tip *If you like, you can save the cheese for sprinkling on top of the pinwheels just before baking.*

F

quick satay

Serves
1

Don't ignore this recipe because you don't believe it really is 'quick'. I've rustled this one up in just five minutes once I've found the tin opener! You can add whatever quick-cooking veg you have around (sweetcorn, spring onion, green beans, etc.) and it's a great recipe for those evenings when you need to get something on the table as quickly as you can.

2 tbsp smooth peanut butter
1 tsp low-salt soy sauce
½ x 400g tin (14oz) of full-fat coconut milk
1 skinless and boneless chicken breast, chopped
½ red pepper, chopped

For cooking

drizzle of sunflower oil

1. Mix together the peanut butter, soy sauce and coconut milk to make the sauce.
2. Heat the oil in a frying pan over a medium heat, add the chicken and fry until golden brown on all sides. Add the pepper and pour over the sauce, then simmer until the pepper has softened. That's it!
3. Serve hot.

F

campfire stew with baked sweet potatoes

Serves
1–2

This is a great dish for all the family and only requires the use of one saucepan, so there's minimal washing up.

- 1–2 sweet potatoes
- 1 rasher of bacon, chopped
- ½ red pepper, chopped
- ½ x 400g (14oz) tin of chopped tomatoes
- ½ x 400g (14oz) tin of baked beans

For cooking

- drizzle of sunflower oil

1. Preheat the oven to 200°C (180°C fan).
2. Bake the sweet potato/es for 40 minutes.
3. Meanwhile, heat a tiny drizzle of oil in a saucepan that has a lid over a medium heat, then add the bacon and fry for a couple of minutes. When the bacon is starting to crisp up, add the pepper and fry for 1 minute, then add the tomatoes and beans. Mix well and reduce the heat down to low, then place the lid on the pan and leave it to simmer for 15 minutes.
4. Slice the baked potato/es in half and spoon the campfire stew over the top to serve.

V F

tomato dal

Serves
2

I often make this when Harry has been a little under the weather because it's full of vitamin C and very comforting. A warm bowl of lentils is good for the soul and leftovers can be used as the base for a soup or simply served as a warm dip with some bread.

180g (1 cup/6oz) red lentils

1 tbsp garlic paste (or 3 finely chopped garlic cloves)

2 handfuls of cherry tomatoes

½ low-salt vegetable stock cube

1. Place all the ingredients in a saucepan with 500ml (2 cups) of water and bring to a simmer over a medium heat. Cook for 20 minutes, stirring occasionally.
2. That really is it!
3. This is lovely served with a hunk of bread for dipping and can be eaten like soup with a spoon.
4. Fine to freeze. Defrost naturally, then reheat in a saucepan to serve.

V

marinara risotto

Serves
4

Simple, honest flavours that work so well together. This is a satisfying yet healthy meal for all the family to enjoy.

190g (1 cup/6½oz) arborio or other risotto rice

4 garlic cloves, minced

1 red onion, finely diced

500ml (2 cups) low-salt vegetable stock

250ml (1 cup) passata

For cooking

drizzle of sunflower oil or knob of butter

1. Add the rice to a saucepan over a medium heat with a little oil or butter and toast the rice for a couple of minutes, stirring constantly. Then add the garlic and onion and a little more butter or oil and stir for a minute. Slowly add the stock, a little at a time, adding more once the rice has absorbed it. Once the stock runs out, slowly add the passata, repeating the same process until the rice is cooked.

2. Once the rice is cooked, leave it to stand for 5 minutes with the heat off before serving. Season, if you wish, and plate up!

V

florentine pizza

Serves
1

There was a time when Harry wouldn't eat spinach. Then, I tried chucking it on a tortilla bread with some cheese and an egg and I called it pizza. I'm sure you can guess what happened next or you wouldn't be reading about it now! I make this for myself and/or Tom for lunch when Harry is at school because we all love it and this is one that Harry actually requests now. Spinach has well and truly been welcomed back into his realm it seems!

1 tbsp cream cheese

1 tortilla wrap

2 handfuls of spinach leaves

1 handful of grated cheese (any type)

1 egg

1. Preheat the oven to 200°C (180°C fan). Line a baking tray with baking parchment.
2. Spread the cream cheese over the tortilla wrap, then sprinkle the spinach in a ring around the outside. Sprinkle the cheese over the whole thing, then crack the egg into the middle.
3. Place the pizza on the prepared tray and bake for 10 minutes.
4. Remove from the oven and leave to cool for a few minutes before serving.

F

creamy chicken & coconut curry

Serves
4

2 skinless and boneless chicken breasts, diced

2 tbsp curry powder

4 tbsp ground almonds

1 x 400ml (14oz) tin of coconut milk

1 handful of raisins

For cooking

drizzle of sunflower oil

A mild and aromatic curry to suit all palates!

1. Add the chicken to a pan over a medium heat with a little oil and the curry powder. Fry until golden.

2. Add the ground almonds and fry until the almonds have coated the chicken. Pour in the coconut milk and add the raisins – turn the heat down to low and simmer for 20 minutes. Turn the heat off, then leave to thicken up for a couple of minutes.

3. Season if you wish before serving.

V

spring risotto

Serves
1

A fresh, vibrant bowl of comforting risotto with lots of green goodness in it. This is a one-pan wonder, so there's minimal washing up and leftovers can be turned into arancini balls (see Tip).

2 spring onions, chopped
95g (½ cup/3½oz) arborio or other risotto rice
285ml (1¼ cups) low-salt vegetable stock
½ courgette, grated
1 handful of peas (fresh or frozen)

For cooking

1 tsp butter or olive oil

1. Heat the butter or oil in a saucepan over a low heat, then add the spring onions and cook until softened.
2. Add the rice and toast it gently. Once you hear it pop slightly and you can smell toasted rice, add the veggie stock. Cook for 10 minutes, stirring the rice every couple of minutes to stop it from sticking. If it starts to catch on the bottom or dry out, add a little splash of water.
3. Add the grated courgette and cook for a further 10 minutes. Add the peas for the final minute to heat through.
4. Serve immediately.

Tip

To make into arancini balls, let the risotto cool. Rub olive oil into your hands and roll the mixture into balls about the same size as golf balls. Take three bowls, crack an egg into one and beat it, add a few tablespoons of plain flour to another, and sprinkle a good handful of breadcrumbs into the third bowl. Take a ball and drop it into the flour, then into the egg mixture and then the breadcrumbs. Repeat this process until all are coated. Shallow-fry them in a little oil over a medium heat until golden and crispy. Pop them on a plate lined with kitchen paper to absorb any excess oil and that's it.

Traybakes & Slow Cooker

V F

veggie lasagne

Serves
4

Lasagne is a staple in lots of houses, but it can be a bit of a faff whipping up a béchamel and a flavoursome Bolognese sauce (without adding mounds of salt), then layering it, etc. This version, however, is very simple and considerably healthier. We often have this as a midweek meal served with chips and salad. Use a loaf tin to make this if you have one, as lasagne sheets fit perfectly inside it and it saves you cutting them to size or layering too many over each other and running the risk of uncooked, chewy pasta.

1 x 100g (3½oz) bag of spinach

1 x 250g (9oz) tub of ricotta

4 lasagne sheets

⅔ x 400g (14oz) tin of chopped tomatoes

1 handful of grated cheese (any type)

1. Preheat the oven to 200°C (180°C fan).
2. Place the spinach in a microwaveable bowl with 2 tablespoons of cold water. Cook on high for 1 minute until soft, then drain.
3. Add the ricotta to the spinach and mix thoroughly.
4. Layer up the lasagne in a 900g (2lb) loaf tin: first, place a layer of pasta sheets, followed by a layer of the spinach mixture, then add a few tablespoons of chopped tomatoes. Repeat until you have used up all your ingredients. Top with the grated cheese.
5. Bake for 40 minutes. Remove from the oven and set aside to firm up for 10 minutes, then slice and serve.

Tip

You can batch make this ahead of time and freeze before cooking. To cook from frozen, add an extra 15 minutes to the cooking time. I don't recommend freezing this once cooked. You can, of course, reheat it from chilled and serve it again within 48 hours if you keep it in the fridge.

V F

mustardy gnocchi bake

Serves
4

This is a great dinner when you just want to bung something in the oven and have a few minutes to yourself. Wholegrain mustard is quite a strong flavour, but the amount required is very tiny. It's a great dish for all the family and is very nice with some fried bacon lardons added to it.

1 packet of gnocchi

1 handful of peas (fresh or frozen)

150ml (⅔ cup) double cream

1 tsp wholegrain mustard

1 handful of grated cheese (any type)

1. Preheat the oven to 200°C (180°C fan).
2. Pour the gnocchi into an ovenproof dish. Sprinkle over the peas, tip in the cream and add the mustard. Mix with a spoon until the mustard and cream are well combined. Sprinkle over the cheese.
3. Bake for 25 minutes.
4. Remove and leave to cool slightly before serving.
5. This is fine to freeze, but I'd be amazed if you have any leftovers! Defrost naturally and then reheat either in the microwave for 30 seconds or pop in a 200°C (180°C fan) oven for 15 minutes.

F

sausage, apple and mango loaf

Serves
4

Meatloaf is a lovely dish to enjoy together and this version is slightly sweet, contains no salt and is very filling, so a little goes a long way. We usually have this with creamy mashed potatoes and some greens and everyone enjoys it. It is also delicious thinly sliced in a sandwich and perfect for picnics.

500g (1lb 2oz) lean pork mince

100g (1 cup/3½oz) porridge oats

2 apples, grated

2 eggs

2 tbsp mango chutney, plus extra for glazing

1. Preheat the oven to 200°C (180°C fan). Line a 22 x 10 x 6cm (8½ x 4 x 2½in) loaf tin with baking parchment.
2. Mix together all the ingredients in a bowl until well combined.
3. Pour the mixture into the prepared tin and level the surface with the back of a spoon.
4. Bake for 45 minutes.
5. Remove from the oven and poke some holes in the top with a fork. Brush a little extra mango chutney over the surface of the loaf and set aside until nearly cool.
6. Slice and serve.
7. If freezing, slice and freeze slices between sheets of greaseproof paper. Defrost naturally and reheat in the oven at 200°C (180°C fan) for 15 minutes.

V F

carrot & courgette tagine

Serves
4

This sweet and spicy one-pot meal is delicious served with warm rice or couscous and a big dollop of thick Greek yoghurt.

2 tbsp harissa

1 x 400g (14oz) tin of prunes, including juice

2 carrots, cut into chunks

1 x 400g (14oz) tin of chopped tomatoes

1 courgette, cut into chunks

1. Preheat the oven to 200°C (180°C fan).
2. Add everything to an ovenproof dish and tightly cover with foil. Place in the oven for 30 minutes, then remove the foil and bake for another 30 minutes, uncovered.
3. Remove from the oven and serve with couscous (optional)!

chorizo alla norma pasta bake

Serves
4

This is seriously delicious. Gorgeous crispy chorizo and soft aubergine with lovely creamy melted mozzarella – heaven!

1 handful of sliced chorizo

1 aubergine, grated

1 x 400g (14oz) tin of chopped tomatoes

300g (11oz) tortellini

1 ball of mozzarella

For cooking

drizzle of sunflower oil

1. Preheat the oven to 200°C (180°C fan).
2. Fry the chorizo in a pan with a little oil, then once it starts to crisp up, add the aubergine and cook until there is no liquid left in the pan and the aubergine is starting to dry up. Once this happens, add the chopped tomatoes and mix thoroughly.
3. Add the tortellini to an ovenproof dish and cover with the sauce. Tear the mozzarella into chunks and scatter them over the top, then tightly wrap the dish in foil. Place in the oven for 15 minutes with the foil covering it, then remove the foil and cook for a further 15 minutes.
4. Finally, remove from the oven and serve!

V F

slow cooker saag paneer

Serves 4

Saag paneer is non-negotiable for me whenever we order a curry; I can't get enough of it. I believe you simply can't have enough garlic in a saag paneer, so as long as everyone else is also eating it – feel free to ignore my recommended, and frankly measly, suggestion of six garlic cloves.

500g (1lb 2oz) spinach leaves

200g (7oz) paneer or halloumi, cubed

2 tbsp garam masala or curry powder

6 garlic cloves, diced

1 x 400g (14oz) tin of coconut milk

1. Add everything to a slow cooker and cook on High for 4 hours.
2. Season if you wish and serve with rice.

V F

butter bean & leek gratin

Serves
4

This is heaven served with a roast chicken! Creamy butter beans with sweet, caramelised leeks and tangy melted cheese – if you're anything like us, this will be something you didn't know you needed until now.

2 leeks, sliced

3 tbsp plain flour

250ml (1 cup) milk

1 handful of grated cheese (any type)

1 x 400g (14oz) tin of butter beans, drained

For cooking

drizzle of sunflower oil

1. Preheat the oven to 200°C (180°C fan).
2. In an ovenproof saucepan or frying pan, add the leeks along with a little oil and fry over a medium heat until they start to colour. Then sprinkle over the flour and stir until combined. Slowly add the milk, whisking constantly until it forms a thick sauce.
3. Finally, turn off the heat and add the cheese and butter beans. Mix thoroughly and transfer to the oven to bake for 30 minutes.

V

greek island aubergines

Serves
2–4

Around ten years ago, I travelled around the Greek Islands, and on one tiny little island I'd never heard of before, Kea, I visited a restaurant where there was no menu. After much struggling to understand each other, the owner disappeared into the kitchen and came back with a baked aubergine covered in tomatoes and feta. It was without doubt the most delicious thing I'd ever eaten! Truly. Smoky aubergine, tart tomatoes, aromatic oregano and tangy baked feta – it's a dish made in heaven.

2 aubergines
500ml (2 cups) passata
4 garlic cloves, minced
2 tbsp dried oregano
1 handful of crumbled feta cheese

For cooking

drizzle of sunflower oil

1. Preheat the oven to 200°C (180°C fan).
2. Slice the aubergines in half lengthways, score the flesh with a knife, pop them in an ovenproof dish lined with baking parchment and drizzle over a little oil. Roast for 30 minutes, skin side down.
3. Remove from the oven and use a fork to gently break apart the flesh inside each aubergine half. Pour some passata over each half, sprinkle over the garlic and oregano and sprinkle the feta over the top.
4. Pop back into the oven and bake for 20 minutes, then remove and serve!

V

garlicky spring green lasagne

Serves
6

I've recommended six to eight garlic cloves here, but if you're anything like me, I always add extra garlic to a recipe, because why wouldn't you? Feel free to use your own judgement on this.

6–8 garlic cloves

2 handfuls of shredded spring greens

500g (1lb 2oz) ricotta

2 handfuls of grated Cheddar

8–12 lasagne sheets

For cooking

drizzle of sunflower oil or knob of butter

1. Preheat the oven to 200°C (180°C fan).

2. Into a frying pan add the garlic, spring greens and a little oil or butter. Sauté for 5 minutes or until the spring greens have become shiny and dark but not crispy and dry, then turn off the heat. Allow to cool for a few minutes, then add the ricotta and most of the Cheddar (save a little to sprinkle over the top). Mix together and season if you wish.

3. Place the pasta sheets across the bottom of an ovenproof dish, not overlapping, to cover the base. Spoon over a quarter of the cheese mixture, then cover with more lasagne sheets and so on, finishing with a layer of cheese mixture on top. Sprinkle the reserved Cheddar on top and bake for 45 minutes.

4. Remove from the oven and leave to stand for 5–10 minutes before slicing.

creamy pepper ravioli with chicken meatballs

Serves
4

Delicious, creamy, super-filling and comforting.

500g (1lb 2oz) chicken mince

1 x 170g (6oz) packet of sage and onion stuffing mix

2 red peppers

300ml (1¼ cups) single cream

300g (11oz) ravioli

For cooking

drizzle of sunflower oil

1. Preheat the oven to 200°C (180°C fan).
2. In a large bowl, combine the chicken mince and stuffing mixture and, using wet hands, roll the mixture into golf-ball-sized balls.
3. Slice the peppers in half from top to bottom, removing the stalks and seeds. Place both the peppers and stuffing balls onto a large baking tray lined with baking parchment and drizzle over a little oil before baking for 30 minutes.
4. Remove from the oven and add the peppers to a food processor along with the cream. Blitz until smooth and season if you wish.
5. Add the sauce to a large saucepan along with the ravioli, pop the lid on top and cook for 5–10 minutes until the ravioli is cooked through. Add the stuffing balls to the pan and mix through to combine.

F

classic cottage pie

Serves
4

Cottage pie. It even sounds like comfort food! Which it is. This is the type of meal you don't have to worry about people not liking, you just pop it down in the middle of the table and everyone sees the gorgeous, thick, brown gravy underneath bubbling up at the sides of a crispy potato top and immediately mouths start watering.

500g (1lb 2oz) potatoes, peeled and chopped

500g (1lb 2oz) beef mince

1 x 400g (14oz) tin of baked beans

300g (2 cups/11oz) frozen mixed veg

1 tbsp Worcestershire sauce

For cooking

drizzle of sunflower oil

1. Preheat the oven to 200°C (180°C fan).
2. Cook the potatoes in a pan of boiling water until soft, then drain and mash them.
3. Add the mince to a frying pan over a medium heat with a little oil and brown off. Then add the beans, frozen veg and Worcestershire sauce, mix thoroughly and cook until heated through. Season if you wish.
4. Transfer the mixture to an ovenproof dish, spreading it out evenly, then top with the mashed potato. Use the back of a fork to get an even top. Bake for 30 minutes, then remove and serve while bubbling and hot!

sausage & hash brown pie

Serves
4

If you've had a difficult day and you just want a hug in a bowl, look no further.

8 sausages, sliced in half lengthways

1 leek, sliced

1 red onion, sliced

150g (5oz) garlic and herb roulé cheese

12 frozen hash browns

For cooking

drizzle of sunflower oil

1. Preheat the oven to 200°C (180°C fan).
2. Add the sausages to a large ovenproof dish along with a drizzle of oil. Bake for 20 minutes, or until the sausages are starting to brown.
3. Remove from the oven and tip over the leek and onion. Dollop the cheese into all the gaps using a spoon. Layer the hash browns over the top and return to the oven for 40 minutes until cooked through and golden brown.

F

corned beef pie

Serves
4

Don't knock it until you've tried it! Cheap as chips to make and completely delicious, this is proper comfort food.

500g (1lb 2oz) potatoes, peeled and diced

1 x 340g (12oz) tin of corned beef

1 leek, sliced

1 tbsp Worcestershire sauce

1 x 400g (14oz) tin of baked beans

1. Preheat the oven to 200°C (180°C fan).
2. Add the potatoes to a saucepan of boiling water and cook until soft. Then drain and mash them.
3. Break the corned beef into chunks and add it to a frying pan along with the leek, then fry over a medium heat for 10 minutes. Add the Worcestershire sauce and baked beans and mix thoroughly.
4. Tip into an ovenproof dish and smooth out. Spoon over the mash and even out the top using the back of a fork. Bake for 30 minutes.
5. Remove from the oven and serve.

V F

cheddar & leek gnocchi bake

Serves
4

Throw it all in a dish and forget about it for twenty-five minutes – this is a real crowdpleaser. Hearty, filling, smells gorgeous in the oven and costs very little to assemble. We have it with a side of sliced pickled gherkins and tomato ketchup. That sounds odd but it really works. Give it a go!

- 500g (1lb 2oz) gnocchi
- 1 leek, sliced
- 1 large red onion, cut into wedges
- 300ml (1¼ cups) single cream
- 2 handfuls of grated Cheddar cheese

1. Preheat the oven to 200°C (180°C fan).
2. Add the gnocchi, leek and onion to an ovenproof dish, pour over the cream and give it a good mix. Sprinkle over the cheese and pop it in the oven for 25 minutes. Then serve up!

salmon & sundried tomato filo pie

Serves
4

No faffing around with pastry cutting or mashing of potatoes, this is a pie you chuck in a dish, scrunch the pastry over the top, then you can stick the TV on for half an hour while it cooks. Easy peasy!

- 4 salmon fillets
- 130g (1 cup/4½oz) frozen peas
- 1 handful of chopped sundried tomatoes
- 300ml (1¼ cups) crème fraîche
- 7–8 sheets of ready-made filo pastry

For brushing

- sunflower oil

1. Preheat the oven to 200°C (180°C fan).
2. Place the salmon in an ovenproof dish, skin side down. Add the peas, sundried tomatoes and crème fraîche. Give it a good mix and season if you wish. Scrunch the pastry sheets on top one at a time to cover. Brush the sheets with a little oil and cook in the oven for 30 minutes

V

mediterranean orzo traybake

Serves
4

Creamy, comforting, easy and filling – you can't go wrong.

100g (1 cup/3½oz) orzo

130g (1 cup/4½oz) frozen peas, defrosted

1 low-salt vegetable stock cube

1 handful of cherry tomatoes

100g (3½oz) feta cheese, crumbled

1. Preheat the oven to 200°C (180°C fan).
2. Add everything to an ovenproof dish along with 500ml (2 cups) of cold water. Cover the dish tightly with foil and bake for 1 hour.
3. Remove from the oven, take off the foil and allow to rest for 5 minutes. Season if you wish before serving.

spicy sausage traybake

Serves
4

This is one I make repeatedly because it's just delicious, plus everybody keeps asking me for it (always a good sign). The mint might sound like an odd afterthought, but it works beautifully and brightens up the whole dish. If you don't want to use harissa, due to its spiciness, you can swap for pesto and then sprinkle basil over at the end.

8 sausages
500g (1lb 2oz) gnocchi
2 handfuls of cherry tomatoes, halved
2 heaped tbsp harissa
1 handful of mint leaves

For cooking

drizzle of sunflower oil

1. Preheat the oven to 200°C (180°C fan).
2. Add the sausages to an ovenproof dish with a little oil and bake for 30 minutes or until they are starting to brown.
3. Remove from the oven and add the gnocchi, cherry tomatoes and harissa. Give it a good mix and bake for another 30 minutes.
4. Once cooked, remove from the oven and sprinkle over the fresh mint before serving.

F

chicken soup pie

Serves
4

This is the perfect dinner for a freezing November evening, when everyone is cold, tired, perhaps a bit grumpy and just wants a bowl of something hot, creamy and comforting. It can also be made in advance, stored in the fridge and popped in the oven for 20 minutes when you get hungry.

2 skinless chicken legs

500g (1lb 2oz) potatoes, peeled and chopped

300g (2 cups/11oz) frozen mixed veg

1 x 400g (14oz) tin of chicken soup

1. Preheat the oven to 220°C (200°C fan).
2. Add the chicken legs to a large ovenproof dish and bake for 40 minutes.
3. Meanwhile, cook the potatoes in a pan of boiling water until soft. Drain, mash and set aside.
4. After the chicken has been in the oven for 40 minutes, remove them and strip the meat from the bone using a fork. Return the chicken to the dish along with the frozen veg and chicken soup and give it a good mix. Spoon the mash over the top and use a fork to even it out. Pop the whole thing back in the oven for a further 20 minutes, then it's ready to serve!

lasagne baked potatoes

Serves
4

This is one of those recipes that sounds like someone should have invented it before now (perhaps they have) because it just works so well! These can be made in advance and popped in the oven for half an hour before serving for a crowdpleasing tea.

- 4 baking potatoes
- 250g (9oz) beef mince
- 3 tbsp tomato purée
- 250g (9oz) ricotta
- 1 handful of grated Parmesan

1. Preheat the oven to 200°C (180°C fan).
2. Pop the potatoes onto a large baking tray and bake them for 1 hour.
3. Meanwhile, brown off the mince in a frying pan over a medium heat, then switch off the heat and add the tomato purée. Mix thoroughly.
4. In a bowl, mix together the ricotta and Parmesan.
5. Remove the potatoes from the oven and slice them in half. Using a spoon, scoop out the potato flesh – being careful not to break the potato skin. Add the potato flesh to the cooked mince and mix together. Season if you wish.
6. Spoon the mince mixture into the empty potato halves, using a spoon to squash down and ensure they are packed in. Finally, top each potato with a tablespoon of the cheese mixture and pop them back in the oven for 30 minutes.
7. Serve hot!

F

sausage & rosemary beans

Serves
4

This is lovely on its own or served with a steaming hot, buttery jacket potato. The addition of rosemary means it smells incredible in the oven and even better when you peel the foil off at the end. What a treat!

6–8 sausages

1 x 400g (14oz) tin of haricot beans, drained

2 carrots, finely diced

1 onion, diced

1 handful of rosemary sprigs

For cooking

drizzle of sunflower oil

1. Preheat the oven to 200°C (180°C fan).
2. Add the sausages to an ovenproof dish with a little oil and bake for 30 minutes or until the sausages are brown and crispy.
3. Remove the dish from the oven and add the remaining ingredients along with a little more oil and place some foil over the top. Bake for another 20 minutes.
4. Then remove from the oven, take off the foil, add a splash of water and give it a good mix to break up the beans. You're ready to serve!

V

harissa halloumi traybake

Serves
4

This is such an easy midweek dinner that we have it often, particularly in the warmer months. For those that like sauce with their potatoes, I recommend mixing a teaspoon of harissa with a good dollop of Greek yoghurt and a squeeze of lemon – mix it together and get dipping!

750g (1lb 10½oz) mini potatoes

2 carrots, sliced

1 handful of Tenderstem broccoli

2 tbsp harissa

1 block of halloumi (225g/8oz), sliced

For cooking

drizzle of sunflower oil

1. Preheat the oven to 200°C (180°C fan).
2. Add the potatoes and carrots to a large ovenproof tray along with a drizzle of oil and bake for 30 minutes.
3. Remove the tray from the oven and add the broccoli along with 1 tablespoon of the harissa paste, then give everything a good mix. Pop the halloumi on top and use a pastry brush to brush the remaining tablespoon of harissa onto the halloumi, then place the whole thing back in the oven for 15 minutes.
4. Remove from the oven and you're ready to eat!

V

baked courgettes

Serves
3–4

These make a lovely light lunch on a summery afternoon. Super-easy to prepare (they don't look it, but they are) and they make for a delicious, healthy meal.

- 3 courgettes
- ½ red onion, finely diced
- 1 handful of cherry tomatoes, halved or chopped
- 1 handful of tinned sweetcorn
- 1 ball of mozzarella, grated

1. Preheat the oven to 200°C (180°C fan).

2. Slice the courgettes in half lengthways and, using a teaspoon, scoop out the flesh from the middle. Add the flesh to a bowl along with the red onion, tomato, sweetcorn and mozzarella. Mix thoroughly and season if you wish.

3. Lay the courgette halves skin side down on a baking tray. Spoon the mixture into the centres (don't worry if they are piled up, they'll flatten into the wells you've made once they are cooked). Cook in the oven for 35 minutes.

V

cheesy veg crumble

Serves
4

When you hear the title and look at the ingredients, you'll probably wonder what on earth I was thinking, but this is comfort food 101 and costs virtually nothing to assemble. You'll just have to try it and see for yourself.

- 130g (1 cup/4½oz) plain flour
- 50g (2oz) softened butter
- 1 handful of finely grated cheese (any type)
- 450g (3 cups/1lb) frozen mixed veg (or any leftover cooked veg that's lying around)
- 1 x 400g (14oz) tin of broccoli and Stilton soup

1. Preheat the oven to 200°C (180°C fan).
2. To a large bowl, add the flour, butter and cheese and bring the mixture together between your fingertips until it resembles breadcrumbs.
3. Add the mixed veg and soup to an ovenproof dish and mix thoroughly to combine. Sprinkle over the crumble mixture and bake for 45 minutes.
4. Remove from the oven and serve up!

F

thai chicken traybake

Serves
4

Oh how I love a traybake – they take all the headache out of cooking for me. Just chuck it all in and get on with something else – it's win-win as far as I'm concerned, and this one is great to plonk down on the table and let everyone serve themselves. You don't even need to worry about plating up for people. Plus, it smells incredible in the oven, so everyone will think you've gone to huge lengths to produce their dinner, when actually you've been reading a book for the past hour (or folding laundry/sending emails/ clearing up toys, etc. – you get the gist).

200g (1 cup/7oz) basmati rice

1 courgette, diced

4 tbsp Thai curry paste

1 x 400g (14oz) tin of coconut milk

6 skinless and boneless chicken thighs

1. Preheat the oven to 200°C (180°C fan).
2. To a large ovenproof dish, add the rice, courgette and half of the curry paste along with the coconut milk and 120ml (½ cup) of cold water. Give it a good mix.
3. Place the chicken thighs on top of the rice and brush them with the remaining curry paste. Cover tightly with foil and place in the oven for 30 minutes. Then remove the foil and bake for a further 30 minutes.

F

ham & courgette torte

Serves
4

I think this is my favourite recipe in the book. It goes into the oven looking like nothing much and comes out looking like a dish of golden, crispy, cheesy goodness with layers of lovely savoury courgette and sweet ham running through it. It's the sort of meal to cheer everyone up a bit.

125g (1 cup/4½oz) breadcrumbs

1 handful of grated Parmesan

2 courgettes, sliced lengthways into long thin strips

100g (3½oz) sliced ham

1 ball of mozzarella

For cooking

drizzle of olive oil

1. Preheat the oven to 200°C (180°C fan).
2. Place the breadcrumbs on a plate along with the Parmesan and mix together. Cover each courgette slice in the breadcrumb mixture by popping it onto the plate and pressing down, then turning over and pressing down again.
3. Lay 3–4 slices of the courgette into the bottom of an ovenproof dish. Then place 3–4 slices of ham on top. Tear a few chunks of mozzarella and pop them in the gaps (don't worry too much about completely filling the gaps). Then add another layer of courgette, followed by ham and mozzarella and so on. Finally, top the whole thing with the remaining breadcrumbs, drizzle a little oil across the top and pop the dish in the oven for 40 minutes.
4. Remove and you're ready to serve!

cajun salmon traybake

Serves
4

This is something I make again and again and again. It's easy, delicious and it looks great. One tray to wash up and everyone has had a hearty meal, which looks impressive but is surprisingly easy to assemble.

750g (1lb 10½oz) new potatoes

2 tbsp Cajun seasoning

4 fillets of salmon

1 handful of asparagus spears

130g (1 cup/4½oz) frozen peas, defrosted and drained

For cooking

drizzle of olive oil

1. Preheat the oven to 200°C (180°C fan).
2. Add the potatoes to a baking tray lined with baking parchment, drizzle with oil and scatter over 1 tablespoon of the Cajun seasoning. Tumble together and then bake in the oven for 30 minutes.
3. While the potatoes cook, add the salmon to a bowl along with a little oil and the remaining Cajun seasoning to marinate.
4. After half an hour of cooking, add the salmon and asparagus to the tray of potatoes. Place in the oven for 12 minutes exactly, then remove. Tip over the peas to warm through and that's it, ready to serve!

Snacks & light bites

F

ham & cheese croquettes

Makes
8–10

Melted cheese, potatoes and ham – you can't go wrong!

400g (14oz) potatoes, peeled and roughly chopped

100g (3½oz) ham, chopped

4 tbsp plain flour

8–10 cubes of Cheddar

1 handful of dried breadcrumbs

For cooking

sunflower oil

1. Cook the potatoes in a large pan of boiling water until soft, then drain and mash them. Set the mash aside to cool for 20 minutes.

2. In a large bowl, add the ham, flour and mashed potato and roll into balls, stuffing a cube of cheese inside each one. Then roll the balls in the breadcrumbs and shallow fry in hot oil until golden and crispy.

SIV-WHIP

V F

cheesy leek puffs

Serves
4

These are a 'must try', even if they don't sound very exciting. Flaky pastry, sweet leeks and creamy cheese! The first time I made these, I took one through for Tom to try and he said it was his favourite of all my recipes.

1 leek, chopped

1 tbsp cream cheese

1 handful of grated cheese (any type)

1 sheet of ready-made puff pastry

For brushing

1 beaten egg or a little milk

1. Place the leek in a small pan of water and boil until soft. Drain and set aside in a bowl until cool.
2. Meanwhile, preheat the oven to 200°C (180°C fan). Line a baking tray with baking parchment.
3. When the leek is cool, mix in the cream cheese and grated cheese.
4. Unroll the puff pastry sheet straight from the fridge and slice it widthways into four rectangles.
5. Spoon the leek and cheese mixture equally among the rectangles, arranging it on just one side of each rectangle and leaving a 1–2cm (½–¾in) border around the edges.
6. Fold over the empty side of the pastry rectangles to cover the filling and use a fork to seal the three open sides. Pierce the top of each parcel with a sharp knife.
7. Pop them on the baking tray and brush with either milk or beaten egg, then bake for 30 minutes.
8. Serve warm but not too hot.

V F

pesto courgette bites

Makes
24

Pesto is a staple ingredient in our house. In fact, I think pesto pasta was my favourite comfort food as a child and Harry shares my love for it! Couscous is wonderfully easy to make and very filling, and this recipe is quick and delicious.

180g (1 cup/5½oz) couscous

½ courgette, grated

1 tbsp green pesto

2 eggs, beaten

For cooking

drizzle of sunflower oil

1. Boil the kettle. Put the couscous in a bowl and add enough boiling water to just cover it. Cover with a plate and steam for 5 minutes.
2. Fluff the couscous with a fork, then stir through the grated courgette and set aside (this will help it cool down quicker).
3. Once the mixture has cooled to lukewarm, stir though the pesto and eggs.
4. Heat a drizzle of oil in a frying pan over a medium heat. Add tablespoon-sized amounts of the courgette mixture, flatten slightly with the back of a spatula until they are about 1cm (½in) thick, and fry for a few minutes on each side until golden.
5. Remove to a plate lined with kitchen paper to absorb any excess oil.
6. We like these dipped in a soured cream and chive dip or spread with a little cream cheese and served cold.
7. Fine to freeze or keep in the fridge for up to 2 days in an airtight container. Defrost naturally, then pop them in a 200°C (180°C fan) oven on a lined baking tray to reheat.

V F

carrot and cashew pesto

Serves
4

This sweet, creamy pesto is a great option for those that love a bowl of pasta. It's full of good fats and vitamin C and is just as nice spread in sandwiches or used as a dip.

2 carrots, peeled and chopped into small chunks

1 handful of cashews

1 handful of grated Parmesan (or vegetarian hard cheese)

juice of ½ lemon

good glug of olive oil

1. Boil the carrots in a pan of water until soft, then drain and set aside until cool.

2. Add the cooked carrots to a blender along with the cashews, Parmesan, lemon juice and olive oil, then blitz until smooth.

3. Store in the fridge and eat within 2 days.

4. It is also fine to freeze. Freeze in small ice-cube trays to quickly thaw when you need a pasta sauce.

V F

pea pinwheels

Serves
4–5

It wouldn't be right to give you a collection of recipes and not include my pinwheels! These are so pretty and delicious and take about two minutes to prepare. You can add extra sweetcorn or peas, if you wish, but we like to keep things simple and serve them like this.

1 sheet of ready-made puff pastry

1 x 300g (11oz) tin of mushy peas

2 handfuls of grated cheese (any type)

For brushing

1 beaten egg or a little milk

1. Preheat the oven to 200°C (180°C fan). Line a baking sheet with baking parchment.
2. Unroll the pastry sheet and spread the mushy peas over the whole sheet all the way to the outsides and corners. Sprinkle the cheese all over the mushy peas.
3. Loosely roll up the pastry sheet into a roll, then slice the roll in swift chops using a sharp knife into discs about 3cm (1¼in) thick. Pop the discs onto the prepared baking sheet, spacing them well apart. Brush each roll with beaten egg or milk.
4. Bake for 30 minutes.
5. Remove from the oven and let them cool for 5 minutes before lifting the pinwheels off the paper.
6. These are fine to freeze. I advise freezing them before baking between layers of baking parchment. They can be baked straight from frozen (add an extra 10 minutes to the cooking time).

V F

broccoli bread

Serves
4

Harry claims his favourite vegetable is, without doubt, broccoli. But guess what Harry almost always turns his nose up at...? Broccoli. I don't understand it either but he certainly loves a slice of broccoli bread, so perhaps this is what he means. Regardless, this makes a great snack because it's very filling and nutritious.

1 head (300g/11oz) of broccoli, finely chopped

1 handful of grated cheese (any type)

100g (1 cup/3½oz) porridge oats

4 eggs

250ml (1 cup) milk (any type)

1. Preheat the oven to 200°C (180°C fan). Grease and line a 22 x 10 x 6cm (8½ x 4 x 2½in) loaf tin with baking parchment.
2. Combine all the ingredients in a bowl and mix thoroughly. Pour the mixture into the prepared loaf tin.
3. Bake for 30 minutes.
4. Remove from the oven and leave to cool in the tin for 5 minutes, then transfer to a wire rack to cool further.
5. Slice and serve.
6. This is fine to freeze, but I advise slicing it before freezing so that you can defrost portions as and when you need them.

Tip *If you fancy vamping it up a little, add a tablespoon of pesto to the mixture as well.*

V F

pizza patties

Makes
12

I call these pizza patties because they taste exactly like little margherita pizzas!

2 wheat biscuits (such as Weetabix)

½ x 400g (14oz) tin of chopped tomatoes

1 tsp tomato purée

1 handful of grated cheese (any type)

4 heaped tbsp self-raising flour

For cooking

drizzle of sunflower oil

1. Crumble the wheat biscuits into a bowl and add the remaining ingredients, except the oil. Mix until well combined.
2. Roll the mixture into balls, each about the size of a golf ball.
3. Heat a drizzle of oil in a frying pan over a medium heat. Add the balls and fry on all sides until golden and crispy (don't worry about squashing them down, they'll do so naturally).
4. Once cooked, pat them with kitchen paper to absorb any excess oil, and serve immediately.
5. Fine to freeze or keep in the fridge for up to 2 days in an airtight container. Defrost naturally and then pop them in a 200°C (180°C fan) oven on a lined baking tray to reheat.

V F

secret cheesy garlic bread

Serves
2

The secret here is that these are secretly packed with veg, completely delicious and so easy to make! You can eat them on their own or pop a plate of them on the table to mop up any leftover pasta sauce at dinnertime.

4 heaped tbsp self-raising flour, or more as needed, plus extra for dusting

2 heaped tbsp low-fat yoghurt, or more as needed

1 handful of grated cheese (any type)

1 cube frozen spinach or 2 handfuls of fresh spinach

1 garlic clove, finely chopped

For cooking

drizzle of sunflower oil

1. Combine the flour and yoghurt in a large bowl, then stir in most of the cheese (saving a little for sprinkling on top).
2. If using frozen spinach, defrost it in the microwave for 1 minute, then drain, chop and leave to cool. If using fresh spinach, cook it in a pan of boiling water for a minute or so until wilted, then drain, chop and cool as above.
3. When the spinach is cool, add it to the bowl and knead together to form a dough. If it's too wet, add a little extra flour; if too crumbly, add a little more yoghurt until you have a nice rollable dough. Split in half and roll out with a rolling pin on a flour-dusted work surface to form two rough circles, about 1cm (½in) thick.
4. Heat a little oil in a frying pan over a medium heat. Add the chopped garlic and, when it is sizzling, add one of the circles of dough. Cook until golden and crispy on one side, then flip and cook the other side. Sprinkle half of the leftover cheese on top to melt while the second side is crisping up.
5. Repeat with the other circle of dough.
6. Serve immediately.
7. Fine to freeze. Defrost naturally and reheat in the microwave for 30 seconds, or eat cold.

F

tortilla tarts

Makes
6

This is one of my 'emergency lunches', as I call them. We have these on those days where we've not got long to eat and I don't want to be faffing around with lots of pans. They might look little but they are really quite filling and they make a great addition to any picnic lunch or snacks to take in the car for a day out.

2 tortilla wraps

1 x 145g (5oz) tin of tuna, drained

6 tbsp chopped tinned tomatoes or fresh tomato

2 eggs

1 handful of grated cheese (any type)

For greasing

butter or sunflower oil

1. Preheat the oven to 200°C (180°C fan). Grease a 6-hole muffin tin with a little butter or oil.
2. Place the tortilla wraps on a chopping board and cut out six discs of the bread, using the tuna tin as a template to cut around. Pop each disc into the holes of the muffin tin.
3. Spoon a tablespoon each of tuna and chopped tomato into each tart.
4. Whisk the eggs in a bowl and divide equally among the tarts.
5. Sprinkle some cheese over the top of each one.
6. Bake for 15 minutes.
7. Remove from the oven and serve.
8. Fine to freeze. Defrost naturally and reheat in the microwave for 30 seconds, or eat cold.

F

cheeseburger pasties

Makes
4

Yes, you read that right, cheeseburger pasties! Filling, utterly delicious, can be eaten hot or cold and they are easy to make in advance – these are a winner.

250g (9oz) beef mince

2 tbsp tomato purée

1 sheet of ready-made puff pastry

1 red onion, sliced into rings

1 handful of grated cheese (any type)

For brushing

1 beaten egg or a little milk

1. Fry the mince in a frying pan over a medium heat for 10 minutes or until it has browned and there is no excess liquid in the frying pan. Add the tomato purée and turn off the heat. Mix thoroughly and season if you wish. Leave it to cool for 15–20 minutes until lukewarm.

2. Preheat the oven to 200°C (180°C fan).

3. Slice the pastry in half vertically, then again horizontally, to make four rectangles. Spoon the mince onto one half of each rectangle. Place a few onion rings on top of the mince, then divide the cheese equally among the four rectangles. Fold over the uncovered side of pastry and use a fork to seal the three remaining sides. Prick a cross into the top of each one to let out any steam using a knife and place them on a tray lined with baking parchment. Brush each pastry with either beaten egg or milk and pop them in the oven for 20 minutes.

4. Remove and leave to stand for 5 minutes before serving.

V F

cheeseboard muffins

Makes
6

A cheeseboard is incomplete without a good dollop of chutney and a few slices of crispy apple, but hang on... what about the crackers?! Well, if you imagine the wheat biscuits here are like crackers, then perhaps it makes sense. These muffins are slightly sweet, slightly salty, slightly acidic and slightly creamy, with crispy edges and soft insides. Yum!

2 apples

1 handful of grated cheese (any type)

2 eggs

1 wheat biscuit (such as Weetabix)

2 tbsp chutney of choice

For greasing

butter or sunflower oil

1. Preheat the oven to 200°C (180°C fan). Grease a 6-hole muffin tin with a little butter or oil.
2. Grate the apples into a bowl, then add the cheese and eggs, and crumble in the wheat biscuit. Mix until well combined.
3. Spoon the mixture equally among the holes of the muffin tin, then spoon a little blob of chutney on top of each one.
4. Bake for 30 minutes.
5. Remove from the oven and leave to cool slightly before popping them out to serve.
6. Fine to freeze and just defost naturally.

V F

bobble patties

Makes
7–8

These are my 'go-to' quick snacks. They are so quick, with the simplest ingredients, and as a family we all love them. I usually cook up a batch, pinch a few myself, give Harry four or five, and Tom eats the leftovers. Then everybody asks for more, so I have to make another batch... I never learn.

½ x 400g (14oz) tin of baked beans

1 handful of frozen peas

1 handful of frozen sweetcorn

3 heaped tbsp self-raising flour

1 handful of grated cheese (any type)

For cooking

drizzle of sunflower oil

1. Mix together all the ingredients, except the oil, in a bowl until well combined.
2. Roll the mixture into seven to eight patties.
3. Heat a drizzle of oil in a frying pan over a medium heat. Shallow-fry the patties for 5 minutes on each side, or until golden and crispy.
4. Pat them with kitchen paper to remove any excess oil and serve.
5. Fine to freeze. Defrost naturally and reheat in the microwave for 30 seconds, or eat cold.

F

curried sausage rolls

Makes
16

Sausage rolls are delicious and kids tend to love them, but they aren't the healthiest thing in the world, plus the shop-bought variety always tends to lack flavour, in my opinion. Making them from scratch could not be any easier, and the addition of curry powder and mango chutney makes a lovely change.

8 sausages
2 tbsp curry powder
1 sheet of ready-made puff pastry
4 tbsp mango chutney

For brushing

1 beaten egg or a little milk

1. Preheat the oven to 200°C (180°C fan).
2. Remove the sausages from their skins and add the meat to a large bowl along with the curry powder. Mix.
3. Place the pastry on a baking tray lined with baking parchment and slice it in half lengthways.
4. Add 2 tablespoons of mango chutney to each piece of pastry and spread all over both.
5. Split the sausage meat in half, adding half to each side of pastry in two long vertical lines down the side of each one.
6. Fold over the other side and use a fork to seal all the edges together. You will have two long sausages at this point. Slice into 5cm (2in) pieces and brush with beaten egg or milk.
7. Bake in the oven for 25 minutes.

V F

pepper & sweetcorn fritters

Makes
6

These are easy to whip up and make a delicious, hearty snack dipped in Greek yoghurt or mayonnaise.

- 1 pepper, diced
- 1 handful of tinned sweetcorn
- 100g (3½oz) feta cheese, crumbled
- 4 tbsp self-raising flour
- 1 egg

For cooking

drizzle of sunflower oil

1. Combine everything in a large bowl and mix thoroughly. Heat a little drizzle of oil over a medium heat. Add the mixture in tablespoon-sized amounts and fry the fritters for 5 minutes on each side.

2. Dab the fritters with a sheet of kitchen towel to absorb any excess oil. That's it!

V

crispy veggie rolls

Makes
12

These might look a bit fiddly to make, but they are actually really simple. They are delicious dipped into some yoghurt or cream cheese.

1 handful of grated carrot

1 handful of chopped kale

3 tbsp cream cheese

1 tsp green pesto

4 sheets of ready-made filo pastry

For brushing

sunflower oil

1. Preheat the oven to 220°C (200°C fan). Line a baking tray with baking parchment.
2. Squeeze any excess liquid out of the grated carrot and place it in a bowl, then add the kale, cream cheese and pesto, and mix together.
3. Place two sheets of the filo pastry on top of each other. Cut them in half horizontally, then cut each half into three equal strips vertically. This should leave you with six equal-sized rectangles. Pop 1 tablespoon of the filling mixture onto each rectangle, then roll them up to enclose the filling as you would a spring roll, sealing them by brushing a little water onto the edges of the pastry.
4. Repeat with the other two sheets of filo and remaining fillling mixture, so you have 12 rolls in total.
5. Pop the rolls on the prepared baking sheet and brush them with oil.
6. Bake for 20 minutes.
7. Remove from the oven and serve hot or cold.

F

pea & bacon patties

Serves
4

Peas and bacon are a combination we know well and it just works. A little salt from the bacon, a little sweetnees from the peas, and then if you add sweetcorn – even sweeter still. Harry loves these literally swimming in ketchup, but I like them just as they are! You can leave out the bacon if you wish and they are still tasty, but I'd recommend adding a little grated cheese or nutritional yeast in its place for flavour.

1 rasher of bacon, chopped
½ x 400g (14oz) tin of mushy peas
1 handful of sweetcorn
2 tbsp self raising flour
1 egg

For cooking

drizzle of sunflower oil

1. Fry the bacon in a dry frying pan until crispy, then set it aside to cool for 10 minutes.
2. When cool, mix the bacon together with all of the other ingredients, except the oil for cooking, in a bowl.
3. Heat the oil in a frying pan over a medium heat. Add tablespoon-sized amounts of the mixture to the pan and fry the patties on both sides for a few minutes until golden.
4. Transfer the patties to a plate lined with kitchen paper and pat them dry and they're ready to serve.
5. These are fine to freeze. Defrost naturally and then reheat in the microwave for 20 seconds.

F

salmon & courgette fishcakes

Makes
8

Fishcakes make a great quick meal or snack and the flavour options are quite literally endless. They are also so easy to make. These are lovely served with a small salad of chopped cucumber drizzled with a little sesame oil and with some white sesame seeds sprinkled on top.

1 x 213g (7½oz) tin of skinless and boneless salmon

1 courgette, grated

2 eggs

4 heaped tbsp self-raising flour

1 tsp low-salt soy sauce (see Tip)

For cooking

drizzle of sunflower oil

1. Combine all the ingredients, except the oil, in a bowl and mix thoroughly.
2. Heat a drizzle of oil in a frying pan over a medium heat. Dollop tablespoon-sized blobs of the mixture into the hot pan and fry until golden brown on both sides. Remove from the pan with a slotted spoon and pat dry with kitchen paper.
3. We like these dipped in ketchup or mayo, or with a salad, as mentioned above.
4. They will keep for up to 48 hours in a sealed container in the fridge. They are also fine to freeze. Defrost naturally and reheat in the microwave or bake on a lined baking tray in a 200°C (180°C fan) oven for 10 minutes.

Tip *If soy sauce is an allergen for your child, cream cheese makes a good alternative here.*

V

chilli cheese quesadilla

Makes
1

Chilli and melted cheese are meant to know each other between bread. I add sliced fresh chilli to mine and dip the finished result in sriracha chilli sauce, but for children, sweet chilli sauce is great because it isn't spicy but it goes really well with cheese.

1 tbsp sweet chilli sauce

1 tortilla wrap

1 handful of grated cheese (any type)

1 spring onion, diced

For cooking

drizzle of sunflower oil

1. Spread the sweet chilli sauce all over the tortilla wrap. Heat a frying pan over a medium heat with a drizzle of oil and pop in the tortilla (dry side down, chilli sauce side facing up).

2. Sprinkle the cheese and the spring onion onto one half of the tortilla. Fold the tortilla in half. Fry for a couple of minutes on one side and then, using tongs, flip the whole thing over and fry for a couple of minutes on the other side (or until gold and crispy on both sides).

3. Tip it out onto a plate and slice into wedges. Serve!

V F

cheesy sprout & butter bean fritters

Makes
10–12

Brussels sprout haters may need to look away! Weirdly, Harry – who used to disregard all things green and remotely healthy – LOVES Brussels sprouts! One of the most divisive vegetables in all the land and my son can't get enough of them. Anyway, combining bitter, earthy sprouts with creamy, buttery beans and tangy melted cheese is so delicious that perhaps even the naysayers might partake. I can't make any promises, but it might be worth a go.

1 x 400g (14oz) tin of butter beans, drained

200g (7oz) Brussels sprouts, shredded

5 tbsp self-raising flour

3 eggs

1 handful of grated cheese (any type)

For cooking

drizzle of sunflower oil

1. In a bowl, mash the butter beans with the back of a fork to form a paste. Add the remaining ingredients and mix together well. Season if you wish.

2. Add a drizzle of oil to a hot frying pan, then add tablespoon-sized amounts of the fritter mixture, spaced apart, and fry on both sides until golden. Dab with a piece of kitchen towel to absorb any excess oil and serve!

Desserts & Sweet Treats

V F

cereal ice cream

Serves
4

I can just imagine your puzzled expression, as it does sound strange, but this recipe was a bit of a breakthrough for me. Harry is borderline obsessed with ice cream, and this healthy version has hit the spot on countless occasions. I usually top it with fresh fruit, arm him with a spoon and wait patiently for the inevitable, 'Mummy, can I have some more please?'

3 ripe bananas
2 wheat biscuits (such as Weetabix)
250ml (1 cup) milk

1. Peel the bananas and add them to a blender along with the wheat biscuits and milk. Blitz until smooth, then pour into a freezerproof container.
2. Freeze for at least 8 hours.

V F

apple crumble tart

Serves
6–8

I love apple crumble and I love apple tart, so it made sense to introduce the two to each other!

1 sheet of ready-made shortcrust pastry

50g (2oz) softened butter

100g (¾ cup/3½oz) plain flour

50g (¼ cup/2oz) brown sugar

1 x 270g (9½oz) jar of apple sauce

For greasing

butter or sunflower oil

1. Preheat the oven to 200°C (180°C fan).
2. Add the pastry to a well-greased 23cm (9in) tart tin and push it gently into all the edges to ensure it fits. Trim the pastry to fit the tin, leaving a few centimetres overhanging all the way around. Using a fork, prick the bottom of the pastry and bake for 10 minutes on its own.
3. Meanwhile, combine the butter, flour and sugar in a bowl and rub together using your fingertips, bringing the mixture together to resemble breadcrumbs.
4. After the pastry has had 10 minutes in the oven, spoon the apple sauce over, making sure it covers the entire pastry base. Sprinkle over the crumble mixture and pop the tin back in the oven for 30 minutes.
5. Remove from the oven and leave to cool for at least 30 minutes in the tin before releasing the tart from the tin and slicing.

V

raspberry & chocolate mousse

Serves
1

Chocolate mousse is probably on most children's pudding wish list, and frankly I don't blame them! However, this version is much healthier and miles easier to make at home. The pectin in the raspberries helps these to set and a few chocolate shavings across the top mean that, if you're anything like me, you'll probably need to photograph this little masterpiece once you've made it, because it looks almost as good as it tastes!

1 handful of raspberries
1 tsp cocoa powder
5 pitted Medjool dates
1 banana
little splash of milk (any type)

To decorate (optional)

chocolate shavings
more raspberries

1. Combine all the ingredients in a blender or food processor and blitz until smooth.
2. Pour the mixture into a small cup or jar and refrigerate for at least 1 hour before serving.
3. Add some chocolate shavings and a raspberry or two to the top to decorate, if you like.

V F

berry jellies

Makes
12

If you are having a little party or perhaps just fancy making something a bit healthier than plain jelly to go with ice cream, then try this recipe. It's also a great way to preserve some fresh berries for a few days longer.

1 packet of jelly (flavour and type of your choice)

1 handful of fresh berries (raspberries work best)

1. Mix up the jelly mixture according to the packet instructions.
2. Pop a berry into each individual section of an ice-cube tray. Pour over the warm jelly mixture and pop the ice-cube tray into the fridge for a minimum of 8 hours to set.
3. That's it!
4. Fine to freeze. Make sure you defrost fully before serving (they are impossible to bite into frozen – I nearly lost a tooth trying – because the outside turns to jelly but the fruit inside stays frozen!).

QUICKKUBE

V F

grape granita

Serves **2**

This started out as a way for Harry to enjoy grapes – which are naturally very sweet and delicious, but they are just about the most well-known choking hazard there is. But I now find that this is a really delicious, simple, natural treat for all the family to enjoy – it's literally JUST grapes!

1 bunch of seedless grapes

1. Pluck all the grapes off the stalks and pop them into a sandwich bag. Freeze overnight or for at least 8 hours.
2. The next day, add them to a blender with 2 tablespoons of water and blitz to combine.
3. Serve immediately.

V F

sweet potato chocolate brownies

Makes 12

The texture of these is similar to that of the most butter-filled, sumptuous brownie you could buy from a farm shop or deli. But that's nothing to do with a complicated process or pounds of unsalted butter – it's the work of that well-known orange superfood, the sweet potato! These are also very nice if you pop them in the freezer and eat them like ice cream!

2 sweet potatoes

2 tbsp coconut oil, softened

130g (1 cup/4½oz) self-raising flour

3 tbsp cocoa powder

3 eggs

To decorate (optional)

melted chocolate

1. Preheat the oven to 200°C (180°C fan). Line a 25 x 16.5 x 3.5cm (10 x 6½ x 1½in) baking tin with baking parchment.
2. Bake the sweet potatoes in the oven for 40 minutes, or until soft.
3. Remove the sweet potatoes from the oven and scoop the flesh out into a bowl. Mash it, then leave it to cool.
4. When cool, add the sweet potato mash to a blender or food processor along with the other ingredients and blitz to combine.
5. Pour the mixture into the prepared tin and bake for 30 minutes.
6. Remove from the oven and leave to cool for 20 minutes before slicing into squares.
7. If you'd like to make these extra sweet, you can drizzle the brownies with melted chocolate when cool.

V F

tropical vegan ice-cream

Serves 12

This is perhaps more a sorbet than an ice cream, but it's absolutely delicious and perfect on a hot summer's day.

½ x 400g (14oz) tin of full-fat coconut milk

2 good handfuls of frozen mango chunks

1. Add both ingredients to a blender and blitz until smooth.
2. That really is it! Serve immediately.
3. Freezes for up to 6 months. Will need to soften for 20 minutes at room temperature before serving.

Tip

You can swap the mango for frozen pineapple, melon, banana or berries.

V F

speculoos banana bark

Serves
4

The perfect snack on a hot afternoon in the garden!

2 bananas

2 tbsp speculoos (such as Biscoff) spread

220g (1 cup/8oz) plain yoghurt

1. Mash the bananas in a bowl and add the speculoos spread, give it a good mix, then add the yoghurt and mix again. Spread the mixture onto a baking tray or dish lined with baking parchment and freeze for a minimum of 4 hours.

2. Using a knife, slice the bark into chunks and serve!

Tip *I always spread extra speculoos on top!*

V F

spiced apple bars

Makes
12

If you want your home to smell like a Danish bakery in the afternoon then I highly recommend these! They really do smell amazing and will certainly stave off any afternoon munchies.

200g (2 cups/7oz) porridge oats

100ml (generous ⅓ cup) milk

2 apples, grated with the skins on

1 banana

1 tbsp mixed spice

For decorating

extra apple, thinly sliced and cut into shapes of your choosing (optional)

1. Preheat the oven to 200°C (180°C fan). Line a baking tin, about 25 x 16.5 x 3.5cm (10 x 6½ x 1½in), with baking parchment.
2. Combine all the ingredients in a bowl until well combined.
3. Spoon the mixture into the prepared tin and squash it down with the back of a spoon. If you like, you can add some apple slices or shapes to the top of each one to decorate.
4. Bake for 30 minutes.
5. Remove from the oven and leave to cool before slicing into squares.
6. Fine to freeze. Defrost naturally before serving.

V F

bramble cheesecake bars

Makes
12

Picking blackberries, or brambles, is a classic way to kill a few hours on a warm late summer's afternoon, but then what do you do with them? This is a great way to use up your surplus and produce a yummy, healthy pudding. If you want to freeze these, they are even less messy, and possibly even better, partially frozen/defrosted as a sort of iced cake bar.

- 6 tbsp unsalted butter
- 2 wheat biscuits (such as Weetabix)
- 3 heaped tbsp cream cheese
- 2 handfuls of brambles (blackberries, raspberries, dewberries)
- 1 tsp raspberry jam

1. Line a dish or tin, about 18 x 11.5 x 4cm (7 x 4½ x 1½in), with baking parchment.
2. Melt 3 tablespoons of the butter in a bowl (either in the microwave or in a pan, then pour into a bowl). Crumble the wheat biscuits into the bowl and mix thoroughly.
3. Pack the mixture into the bottom of the lined dish and use the back of a spoon to flatten it.
4. Pop the dish in the fridge for 10 minutes to set.
5. Meanwhile, combine the remaining 3 tablespoons of butter in a separate bowl with the cream cheese, brambles and jam until well combined.
6. Spoon the mixture on top of the wheat-biscuit base and smooth it out.
7. Freeze for at least 2 hours, then slice into squares to serve.
8. These will keep for up to 48 hours in the fridge in a sealed container, but they will be very soft. For a firmer bar, they are fine to freeze. Remove from the freezer a few minutes before you want to serve them – they are nice to eat while still partially frozen as a sort of ice-cream bar.

V

whipped mandarin 'mousse'

Serves
4

Kids love mousse – they go nuts for the stuff! But the amount of sugar in them is usually eye-watering when you think how unfulfilling a little pot of mousse actually is! This version is much more satisfying and significantly healthier – plus, with only two ingredients to worry about, they're incredibly easy to make!

250g (9oz) mascarpone

300g (11oz) tinned mandarin segments in syrup, drained and syrup reserved

1. Place the mascarpone and mandarin segments in a food processor and blitz until smooth. Pour the mixture into individual glasses or bowls and leave to set in the fridge for at least a couple of hours.

2. Serve either with some of the syrup poured over the top or save it to add to a fruit salad.

V F

cheat's peach custard tart

Serves
4

A delicious crowdpleasing dessert that looks as pretty as a picture.

1 sheet of ready-made shortcrust pastry

1 x 400g (14oz) tin of custard

2 eggs

1 x 400g (14oz) tin of sliced peaches, drained

For greasing

butter or sunflower oil

1. Preheat the oven to 200°C (180°C fan).
2. Add the pastry to a well-greased 23cm (9in) tart tin and push it gently into all the edges to ensure it fits. Trim the pastry to fit the tin, leaving a few centimetres hanging over the edge all the way around. Using a fork, prick the bottom of the pastry and bake for 10 minutes on its own.
3. While the pastry is in the oven, combine the custard and eggs in a jug and give it a good mix until combined.
4. Once the pastry case has been in the oven for 10 minutes, remove it and pour in the custard mixture. Arrange the peaches across the top and add it back to the oven for 45 minutes.
5. Remove from the oven and leave to cool in the tin for 30 minutes before removing from the tin and slicing.

Tip *If you are using peaches in syrup, you can save the syrup to drizzle over at the end.*

V F

banana fritters

Serves
4

These are really rather good with a dollop of vanilla ice cream!

1 egg

130g (1 cup/4½oz) self-raising flour

175ml (¾ cup) milk

3–4 bananas

4 tbsp golden syrup

For cooking

drizzle of sunflower oil

1. In a large bowl, combine the egg, flour and milk and whisk until smooth.
2. Peel and slice the bananas into diagonal strips (about 1cm/½in thick). Drop the banana slices into the batter, then add them one by one to a frying pan over a medium heat with a drizzle of oil. Fry each piece on both sides until golden and then remove from the pan.
3. Once the banana pieces have all been cooked, turn the heat down to low and add them back to the frying pan along with the golden syrup. Once the syrup starts to foam and bubble, remove them and plate up!

GOLDEN SYRUP

V F

peanut butter fudge

Makes
8

200g (7oz) white chocolate

125g (½ cup/4½oz) peanut butter

This is so easy and delicious, it should be illegal!

1. Melt the chocolate in a microwaveable bowl in the microwave for 2 minutes (or until melted), stopping every 30 seconds to stir.

2. Once the chocolate is melted, combine it with the peanut butter and mix thoroughly. Pour the mixture into a dish or container lined with baking parchment and smooth it out. Pop it in the fridge for at least 1 hour.

3. Once set, remove the fudge from the freezer, peel off the parchment and slice into chunks.

V F

no-churn raspberry & white chocolate ice cream

Serves
4–6

When I first made this, I didn't tell Tom and Harry that it was homemade and Tom asked me what brand it was because it was so delicious. He didn't believe me when I said I'd made it!

300ml (1¼ cups) double cream

1 x 400g (14oz) tin of condensed milk

1 handful of raspberries

1 handful of white chocolate chips

1. Whip the double cream in a large metal bowl until it forms stiff peaks. Slowly add the condensed milk and mix thoroughly.
2. Fold the raspberries and chocolate into the mixture, then add it to a freezerproof container and freeze for a minimum of 8 hours.

V F

banana bread

Serves
4–6

The riper the bananas, the more delicious this is! With just three ingredients and absolutely no added sugar, this is a great alternative to banana bread as we know it. It doesn't crumble like traditional cake so it's the perfect texture to hold.

3 ripe bananas
4 wheat biscuits (such as Weetabix)
4 eggs

1. Preheat the oven to 200°C (180°C fan). Line a 22 x 10 x 6cm (8½ x 4 x 2½in) loaf tin with baking parchment.
2. Mash two of the bananas in a bowl, then crumble in the wheat biscuits. Add the eggs and mix together until well combined.
3. Pour the mixture into the prepared tin. Slice the final banana lengthways and place it on top of the mixture.
4. Bake for 25 minutes, or until a skewer inserted into the loaf comes out clean (it may need another 5 minutes).
5. Remove from the oven and leave to cool before slicing.
6. If freezing, slice and freeze individual slices between sheets of baking parchment. Defrost naturally and pop in the microwave for 20 seconds, or eat cold.

V F

fruit lollies

Serves
4

These aren't sugar-free, of course, but make a lovely refreshing snack. They look just like chocolate lollies, but include a lot more goodness. Watermelon is probably up there as a favourite fruit for lots of people, but they are absolutely enormous and impossible to store if you buy them whole, or gone in seconds if you buy the snack pots or packets. This way, you can eke out those precious slices for a little longer or preserve the leftovers if you've invested in a whole one, and pack your freezer with healthy lollies for many desserts to come! I use pre-sliced watermelon fingers for this. You can buy them in most supermarkets and they are deseeded, which makes things much easier.

100g (3½oz) white or milk chocolate, as you like

1 tbsp coconut oil

lollipop sticks

watermelon fingers (bought ready-sliced or make your own cut into 10 x 2 x 2cm/4 x ¾ x ¾in sticks)

1. Place the chocolate and coconut oil in a microwaveable bowl. Melt in the microwave on high power for 1 minute, pausing every 20 seconds to stir it.
2. Insert a lollipop stick into one end of each watermelon finger.
3. Once the chocolate is melted, dip each watermelon finger in the chocolate and turn until coated.
4. Pop each lolly on a plate covered in clingfilm and freeze for a minimum of 8 hours.

Tip *I also love to make mango lollies in exactly the same way. So pretty!*

V F

lemon curd cheesecake

Serves
6–8

I'm fairly obsessed with lemon curd; I have to restrain myself from spooning it out of the jar and directly into my mouth. However, I think this is a much better use of it. This luxurious cheesecake is sure to put a smile on everyone's face.

200g (7oz) digestive biscuits

100g (3½oz) butter, melted

300ml (1¼ cups) double cream

500g (1lb 2oz) cream cheese

320g (1 cup/11½oz) lemon curd, plus extra (optional) to serve

1. Put the digestives in a sandwich bag and smash to crumbs using a rolling pin. In a large bowl, combine the crushed biscuits with the melted butter and mix thoroughly.

2. Line the base of a loose-bottomed 20cm (8in) cake tin with baking parchment, pour in the biscuit mixture and flatten evenly across the bottom using the back of a spoon. Pop the tin in the fridge for 30 minutes to set the biscuit base.

3. Meanwhile, add the double cream to a bowl and, using an electric whisk, whip until it forms stiff peaks. Then add the cream cheese and lemon curd and give it another whizz until the mixture is fluffy and thick.

4. Once the base has had 30 minutes in the fridge, spoon the lemon mixture over the base and use a spoon or spatula to smooth it to a nice even top. Place the whole thing back in the fridge for at least 1 hour before gently prising the cheesecake out of its tin. Swirl some extra lemon curd on top, slice and serve!

Tip *If you want to make sure this dessert is vegetarian, use veggie lemon curd that has no gelatin.*

Conversion *Charts*

Liquid measures

Metric	Imperial
1.25ml	¼ tsp
2.5ml	½ tsp
5ml	1 tsp
15ml	1 tbsp
30ml	1fl oz (2 tbsp)
50ml	2fl oz
75ml	3fl oz
100ml	3½fl oz
125ml	4fl oz
150ml	5fl oz (¼ pint)
175ml	6fl oz
200ml	7fl oz
250ml	8fl oz
275ml	9fl oz
300ml	10fl oz
325ml	11fl oz
350ml	12fl oz
375ml	13fl oz
400ml	14fl oz
450ml	15fl oz (¾ pint)
475ml	16fl oz
500ml	18fl oz
600ml	20fl oz (1 pint)
700ml	25fl oz (1¼ pints)
850ml	30fl oz (1½ pints)
1 litre	35fl oz (1¾ pints)
1.2 litres	40fl oz (2 pints)
1.3 litres	2¼ pints
1.4 litres	2½ pints
1.75 litres	3 pints
2 litres	3½ pints
3 litres	5 pints

Spoons

1 tsp	5ml
1 dsp	10ml
1 tbsp (3 tsp)	15ml

Dry weights

Metric	Imperial
10g	¼oz
15g	½oz
20g	¾oz
25g	1oz
40g	1½oz
50g	2oz
60g	2¼oz
70g	2¾oz
75g	3oz
100g	3½oz
115g	4oz
125g	4½oz
140g	4¾oz
150g	5oz
160g	5½oz
175g	6oz
200g	7oz
225g	8oz (½lb)
250g	9oz
275g	9½oz
300g	11oz
350g	12oz
375g	13oz
400g	14oz
425g	15oz
450g	16oz (1lb)
500g	1lb 2oz
550g	1¼lb
600g	1lb 5oz
675g	1½lb
725g	1lb 10oz
800g	1¾lb
850g	1lb 14oz
900g	2lb
1kg	2¼lb
1.1kg	2½lb
1.25kg	2¾lb
1.3kg	3lb
1.5kg	3¼lb

Meal Planner *Template*

Here is a handy meal planner template. Ideal for planning out your own menus, once you've worked out what works for your family. Photocopy it and stick it to your fridge for easy reference.

	M	T
Breakfast		
Lunch		
Dinner		
Dessert		

W	Th	F	Sat	Sun

Index

Acknowledgements

Firstly, I'd like to thank YOU, the lovely person reading this book. I don't know how you came across me and my recipes but I'd hazard a guess it might be social media related and that means a lot. To trust a stranger on the internet enough to cook something I came up with, and then feed it to your families – will never NOT baffle, amaze and delight me. So, thank you, from the bottom of my heart.

I'd like to thank my lovely team at HQ, especially Louise McKeever, who came back from maternity leave with a bang and here we are with this VERY book! She is the most approachable person in publishing and has been beyond patient with me and my 'sometimes replies within five minutes' or 'maybe not for a month' strategy to life and business (I don't think my '5 steps to success' podcast is going to get off the ground anytime soon..) Having just had a little one herself, I think she gets it, but it's always appreciated.

I wouldn't have written one, let alone four books, were it not for the unwavering support and cheerleading from the wonderful Juliet. My equally patient and truly brilliant literary agent. Juliet puts up with me much like the owner of a labrador does. I tend to wander off, then return fizzing with excitement for no discernible reason. But much like a labrador, I'm fiercely loyal to her and we make a great team.

To the very talented Liz and Max who shot every single photo you see here and to Rosie and her team who cooked everything to make it far more beautiful than I ever could. The shoots are one of the best bits about making a book, everyone from all aspects of the process comes together to exchange ideas and funny stories over a banquet of food and decent coffee. It's heaven actually.

And finally, to my family. And specifically, to Tom, for caring about food more than anyone I know (perhaps even me) – our shared love of food and talking about it makes my career a doddle really. We share ideas, we plan a life around food, we live the life we have because of it. This would have been a much trickier path to tread if there was only me to propel this whole thing forwards, luckily, I have a very knowledgeable team mate to navigate it with. One who tells me precisely what he thinks without mincing his words (direct would be an understatement) so if a recipe passes the 'Tom-test' it's probably here. And there's plenty that don't! Quality control if you like. He might prefer the term 'manager.' But I don't think we'll let that one slide under the rug or the power might get to him and then what next? If I unexpectedly publish a handbook on how best to cook offal, then you know exactly what's happened and send help immediately! To the man who makes me laugh through it all and always says, 'just go for it' whenever I have an idea – thank you.

When using kitchen appliances please always follow the manufacturer's instructions.

HQ
An imprint of HarperCollins*Publishers* Ltd
1 London Bridge Street
London SE1 9GF

www.harpercollins.co.uk

HarperCollins*Publishers*
Macken House
39/40 Mayor Street Upper
Dublin 1
D01 C9W8
Ireland

10 9 8 7 6 5 4 3 2 1

First published in Great Britain by
HQ, an imprint of HarperCollins*Publishers* Ltd 2026

Grace Mortimer asserts the moral right to be identified as the author of this work.

A catalogue record for this book is available from the British Library.

ISBN: 9780008650322

Photographer: Haarala Hamilton Photography
Design Direction: Nic & Lou
Layout Designer: James Boast
Publishing Director: Louise McKeever
Assistant Editor: Lian Wilson
Production Controller: Noemi Vallone

Printed and bound in Malaysia by Papercraft

MIX
Paper | Supporting responsible forestry
FSC www.fsc.org FSC® C007207